BÉARA

RESCUED FOLKLORE, HISTORIES AND SONGS FROM IRELAND'S SOUTH-WEST

VOLUME 2

Mike Baldwin

First published in Great Britain in 2025
Copyright © Mike Baldwin, 2025
Bright Light Books
ISBN: 978-1-0369-0576-7

www.mike-baldwin.net

Cover design © Mike Baldwin, 2025
Cover image: Richard John Griffith, A General Map of Ireland to
Accompany the Railway Commissioners (Dublin: Hodges & Smith, 1839).

Transcribed from the School's Collection with the kind permission of the
National Folklore Commission, University College Dublin.
https://www.duchas.ie/en

ALSO AVAILABLE

Mizen: Rescued Folklore, Histories and Songs from Ireland's South-West

ISBN: 9781399921602

Skibbereen: Rescued Folklore and Histories from Ireland's South-West

ISBN: 9781399917049

Béara: Rescued Folklore, Histories and Songs from Ireland's South-West (Vol. 1)

ISBN: 9781036904449

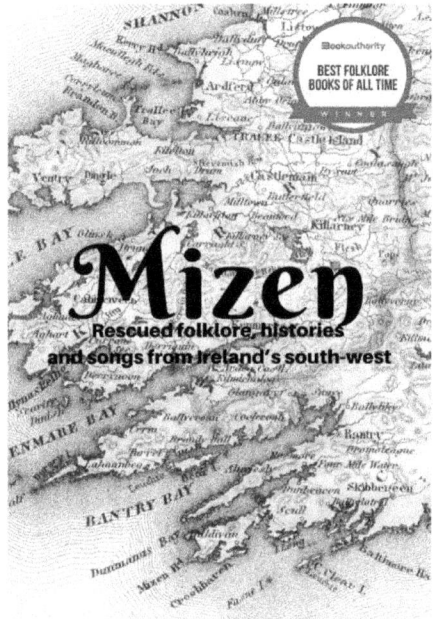

BEST FOLKLORE
BOOKS OF ALL TIME
WINNER

Mizen
Rescued folklore, histories
and songs from Ireland's south-west

Mike Baldwin

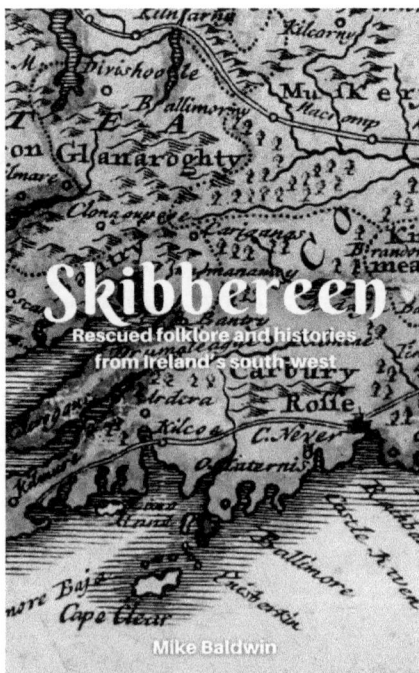

Skibbereen
Rescued folklore and histories
from Ireland's south west

Mike Baldwin

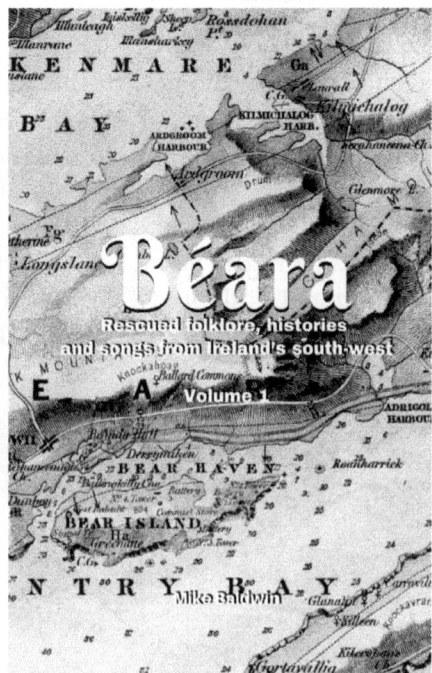

Béara
Rescued folklore, histories
and songs from Ireland's south-west
Volume 1

Mike Baldwin

Editor's Note

This is the second volume of Béara: Rescued Folklore. When writing the first book it became clear that there was too much material for one volume alone. This volume covers schools on the northern side of the Béara. Like volume 1, it is transcribed from materials written by the school children of the Béara Peninsula between 1937 and 1939. Again, syntax and grammar have been preserved, representing the voices of the Béara people at that time. English spellings have been corrected and punctuation added only where necessary to ensure clarity. Irish spellings, whilst sometimes non-standard, have also been maintained.

Acknowledgements

I would like to thank those who have patiently given me space during the writing of this book, and to those who have read it and made suggestions. Special credit is due to my grandmother and parents for introducing me to West Cork, especially to our family home in Goleen; to those in Goleen who have encouraged the writing of the first three Rescued Folklore books, *Mizen: Rescued Folklore, Skibbereen: Rescued Folklore,* and *Béara: Rescued Folklore (volume 1).*

This book is dedicated to the children of West Cork and Kerry who so diligently collected their folklore.

Contents

INTRODUCTION

The Béara Peninsula, with its dramatic landscapes and wind-swept cliffs, cradles a unique history that bridges Ireland's ancient and modern worlds. For centuries, this rugged corner of the South-West has been a place of resilience and mystery, shaped by its harsh beauty, isolated communities, and the unyielding Atlantic Ocean. This volume, the second in a series dedicated to rescuing and preserving the folklore, histories, and songs of Béara (and fourth in the Rescued Folklore series) invites readers to immerse themselves in the voices of a bygone era—voices that echo the rhythms of this land and its people.

Between 1937 and 1939, Ireland's National Folklore Commission embarked on an ambitious project known as the Schools' Collection. Schoolchildren across the country became amateur folklorists, gathering oral histories, legends, and traditions from their parents, grandparents, and neighbours. For the Béara Peninsula, this initiative became an act of cultural preservation, capturing the stories and songs of a people whose lives were deeply entwined with their surroundings. These children, armed with notebooks and pencils, became the bridge between an oral past and a written future, ensuring that Béara's heritage would not fade into the shadows of modernisation.

This book is more than a collection of folklore; it is a time capsule. It offers a glimpse into a world where the supernatural was never far away, where practical wisdom shaped everyday life, and where the boundaries between myth and reality blurred. Béara's inhabitants, like those in many rural Irish communities, lived in an intimate relationship with the land and sea. Their stories reveal a profound understanding of the natural world and a belief in forces beyond human control—be they spirits, fairies, or the mercurial weather that shaped their lives. These tales, transcribed from the voices of farmers, fishermen, blacksmiths, and homemakers, are imbued with humour, reverence, and an enduring sense of wonder.

To understand the folklore of Béara, one must first understand the land itself. The peninsula is a tapestry of contrasts: towering mountains loom over lush valleys; ancient stone ruins dot the windswept moors; and the vast Atlantic stretches endlessly beyond the jagged coastline. It is a place where history speaks from every stone, from the Bronze Age copper mines of Allihies to the medieval castles and ring forts scattered across the landscape. The geography of Béara is not merely a backdrop to its stories; it is a central character, shaping the lives and imaginations of its people.

The sea, in particular, plays a dominant role in Béara's folklore. As both a provider and a threat, the ocean was an ever-present force in daily life. Fishermen risked their lives to reap its bounty, while storms and shipwrecks brought tales of tragedy and survival. The stories collected here often reference these maritime connections, offering glimpses into a community that understood the sea as a source of sustenance, mystery, and danger.

Béara's mountains and valleys are equally significant. They provided shelter and sustenance but also carried an air of otherworldliness. Legends of fairy forts, hidden treasures, and enchanted creatures abound, reflecting a deep-seated belief in the unseen. These landscapes were not just physical spaces; they were imbued with meaning and memory, places where the past lingered and the supernatural could break through into the mundane.

The tales in this collection are more than entertainment; they are a form of history. In a time when written records were scarce, storytelling was the primary way communities preserved their knowledge and identity. The stories passed down through generations encapsulate the values, fears, and aspirations of the people who told them. They offer insights into how Béara's inhabitants understood their world—whether through practical weather lore, rituals for good fortune, or cautionary tales about meddling with fairy lands.

Many of the narratives collected by the schoolchildren reveal the enduring scars of Ireland's turbulent history. The Famine, for instance, looms large in the collective memory, its devastating impact captured in both explicit accounts and allegorical tales. Stories of evictions, emigration, and hardship reflect a community shaped by loss but also resilience. Through these stories, readers can trace the interplay between historical events and the imaginative worlds they inspired.

One of the most striking aspects of Béara's folklore is the coexistence of Christian and pre-Christian beliefs. Saints and spirits inhabit the same landscape, their stories intertwining in ways that reflect Ireland's layered heritage. Holy wells, for example, are places of both Christian pilgrimage and older pagan reverence. Similarly, the fairies of Irish folklore—sometimes benign, often capricious—appear in many tales, their presence accepted as a matter of fact in the lives of Béara's people. These beliefs were not merely theoretical; they shaped behaviour and decision-making. Farmers avoided disturbing fairy forts, knowing that to do so might invite misfortune. Fishermen observed rituals before setting out to sea, and families followed intricate customs to protect their homes from harm. This blending of the sacred and the supernatural created a worldview in which every action had significance, every place a story, and every moment a connection to something larger.

Songs, too, are an essential part of Béara's heritage. They served as a means of entertainment, education, and emotional expression. Whether sung at gatherings, during work, or in solitude, these songs carried the joys and sorrows of the community. They often blended local events with universal themes, creating a shared sense of identity. In this volume, readers will find songs of love and loss, triumph and tragedy, each one a window into the soul of Béara.

The act of storytelling itself was a communal experience. Around the hearth on long winter nights, neighbours would gather to share tales, forging bonds and passing on traditions. These gatherings were not just about preserving stories; they were about creating connections. By sharing their lives through words, Béara's people built a sense of belonging that transcended individual struggles.

As we read these stories today, it is important to recognise the fragility of oral traditions. Without the intervention of the National Folklore Commission and the dedication of the schoolchildren who collected these tales, much of this rich heritage might have been lost. The voices captured in this book remind us of the importance of preserving cultural memory, not only for its historical value, but for the insights it offers into who we are and where we come from.

In transcribing these accounts, care has been taken to preserve the original syntax and phrasing, reflecting the authentic voices of Béara's people. While some spellings and punctuation have been standardised for clarity, the heart of the stories remains untouched. They are presented here not as relics of the past but as living connections to a vibrant cultural tradition.

This volume is both a celebration and an invitation. It celebrates the resilience and creativity of the Béara Peninsula, its people, and its stories. At the same time, it invites readers to become part of this tradition by engaging with the tales, imagining the landscapes, and perhaps even sharing the stories with others. In doing so, we honour the storytellers who came before us and ensure that their voices continue to resonate for generations to come. As you turn the pages of this book, may you feel the spirit of Béara—a place where the past is never far away, where every hill and valley hold a secret, and where the simple act of telling a story keeps a culture alive. Welcome to Béara. Let the journey begin.

Mike Baldwin, April 2025

CLOAN

Co. Chorcaighe
Bar: Béara
Par: Cill na Manach
Scoil: An Chluain
Oide: Tadgh Ó Cearbhaill

CLOAN
Local Folklore and Stories

The Great White Bear

One night long ago two men were returning to their homes in this parish from a fair which was held in Castletownbere. They were about half-ways home and were crossing a bridge. One of the men said to the other. "Some people would be afraid to pass this bridge in the night-time, as for me I do not know what fear is."

"I am not a coward either said the other, I am known to be one of the bravest men in the parish." Just then, they heard a slight noise in a thicket a few feet away from them and looking around quickly they saw the form of an animal.

"What is that" said one man as he grabbed his friend's arm.

"A bear," cried the other, "a great white bear run for your life." And run they did, uphill and down dale until they came to the village of Cluin. They quickly spread the alarm and the inhabitants of the village ran to them to know what all the fuss was about. "A bear, a great white bear," they cried and spoke as fast as they could. "We were just passing through Clíathán An Ré," said one man, "when there close behind us we saw some terrible monster. It is as big as a calf, and as white as snow."

"I saw it first" said the other but I did not run away till my companion here did."

The people said they would go at once and kill the bear. The men took axes, hammers, and guns. The women went with brooms and mops. As the crowd drew near to the bridge no one wanted to go first. The two men who saw the bear were asked to lead the way, but they hung back. At last, one boy with a gun in his hand walked bravely in front. He had but a few steps taken when out from the bushes walked an old white sheep. Then how the people laughed and laughed, but for the two men who saw the bear, it is not told whether they laughed or not.

Informant: Cornelius O'Sullivan, Coominches, Allihies, Co. Cork

The House of the Dead

About thirty years ago a man named Patrick Lowney from Locánmore was coming home from Cahermore. When he came to Kill Ough he saw a house. He went into the house and there were people inside. He knew some of them, but those he knew were all dead people. There was a churn making in the house, so he twisted the churn a few times. After some time, they laid the table and got tea ready. Meanwhile a girl came downstairs. It seemed to the man that she was his own daughter. This girl went to the man and told him, that the people of the house would ask him to take tea and that he would be forced to take it. The others did not hear the girl saying this. There was another man with this man also. When they heard what the girl said, the two of them got up and went out and went on their journey home.

Collector: Máire Ní Murchadha, Allihies, Co. Cork
Informant: Seán Ó Murchadha, 85 years, farmer

St Patrick and Oisin

Long ago, in the year 432, Oisin who had been in Tir-Na-nOg came to Ireland. Once he came to this place riding on his milk white steed. He met a girl who had a horse. She was putting a half sack of flour on the horse. Oisin was a very strong man, so he caught the bag while on his horse and threw it from the ground on the horse's back with one hand. It fell down on the other side again. He then jumped off his milk white steed. As soon as he put his foot on the ground, he got old, feeble, and grey.

Meanwhile St Patrick came to him and was teaching Oisin all about God and what a powerful and strong man God was. Oisin then said to St Patrick: "Dá bhfeichfinn Scor (sé sin mac do Oisin) agus Dia lámh ar láimh ar gCnoc na bFionn agus da bfeichfinn Scor ar lár déarfainn gur fear laidir Dia" ["If I saw Scor (that's Oisin's son) and God hand in hand on Knoc na bFinn and if I saw Scor in the middle I would say that God is a strong man"].

The Norman Ship

During the time of the Norman invasion in Ireland it is said a Norman ship came into Ballydonegan Bay. When it came the people were at Mass. One man who was going to the church saw the ship. When he reached the church, he told the priest and the people who were assembled there about the strange ship which had entered the harbour. When the priest saw it, he knew immediately that it was a Norman ship and that before long it would land, and the Normans would plunder and destroy the district. He told the people to pray, so as that the ship would not succeed in landing. He then took a crucifix in his hand and made the sign of the cross facing the sea and prayed at the same time. The ship immediately sank and was never seen again. Some of the cargo which she had on board was washed into the neighbouring strands. Large quantities of flour and meal and many other articles were found, and to this day, the cave near which the ship was wrecked is called Cúas Na Normánaig, and it's also said that the ghosts of the Norman sailors who were drowned still haunt the cliffs and caves along the shore of Ballydonegan Bay.

Collector: Diarmuid Ó hArrachtáin, Cahermeeleboe, Co. Cork
Informant: Diarmuid Ó hArrachtáin, aged 88, farmer

The Glas Gaibhneach

Long ago there was a blacksmith living on a small farm in Garnish. The landlord evicted him, and he went to live on a small island southeast of Dursey Island. Here he built a forge and he worked for the people of the parish. He prayed to God each morning and evening for a cow. One morning when he arose, he saw a green cow coming towards him from the sea. He drove her back twice, but she came back each time. It was published all through the parish, but nobody came for the cow, so the smith kept her. This cow was a great milker and could fill any vessel that the smith had. Sometimes the cow went to a field in Dingle or to a field in Garnish, and sometimes she stayed on the island. About a year after he got the cow he got married. One day when he was out of home the cow came to be milked and while she was being milked an old woman came to the smith's wife and said, "I have a vessel that your cow cannot fill." So, the smiths wife told her to get it. The old woman went away and returned in five minutes with a strainer. The cow was milked into the strainer but no matter how fast the cow gave her milk she could not fill it. She gave so much milk that she dropped dead. Immediately that she dropped six mermaids came and took her to the sea.

Collector: Sighle Ní Súílleabháin, Cloan, Co. Cork
Informant: Diarmuid Ó hArrachtáin, aged 88, farmer, Cahermeeleboe, Co. Cork

The Shaft at Coom

Once upon a time there were three men working in a shaft in Coom. The shaft is situated in the farm of Michael Sullivan which is about a mile from the village of Cluin. These men were looking for copper. In the early hours of the morning one of the men went to the store house for some powder. As he came closer to the door, he was struck back by a great noise, so he returned back to his companion and told him of the noise which he had heard. They both went back to the powder store, and they managed to get the powder alright. It was a custom by the men who used drills to bring them to the forge to be sharpened so as to have them ready for the next crowd of men who were to use them. The forge was situated in the upper end of the village of Cluin. One day two men were coming to the forge and when their journey was nearly completed, they were attacked by a small dog who kept constantly barking at them. One man went to the forge and the dog was still barking at the other man so much so that he had to remain with his back against the fence until the other man returned. The little dog disappeared in Poll Buidhe and he was never seen since. The next morning when they went to their work, they weren't long there when the man that the dog attacked was killed instantly.

Collector: Sighle Ní Súílleabháin, Cloan, Co. Cork
Informant: Seán Ó Leamhna, aged 63, fisherman

The Priest and the Spirit

Long ago a Reentrisk man and his son were coming home from Castletown by a short cut across the hill. Another man told him that there was an evil spirit in the hill, but he said he did not believe him. So, they went across the hill. When they reached a place called the Caiseac they saw something like a pig coming towards them. The pig attacked the boy and no matter what the man did he could not stop him. The pig killed the boy and went away. The man brought the boy home on his back and sent for the priest. When the priest arrived, he sent all the people out and sometime in the evening when they went back the boy was alright. The priest went to the Ciseac and the spirit appeared in the form of a woman. The priest made a ring around her with holy water and then he asked the spirit why she appeared. The spirit said that she had killed an unbaptised baby. The priest then said some prayers and the spirit disappeared and she was never seen again.

The Murphy Brothers and the Sunfish

Long ago when the Coom mine was working there were two men living in Barness named Mike and Jim Murphy. They lived on fishing and four acres of land. They had three goats on the land, and they grew oats, wheat, and potatoes. One year they made a lot of money at the fishing and Jim said, "We'll buy a boat, Mike." "Alright," said Mike, "I'll be the captain as I'd be the best." So, they bought the boat and went out fishing every morning and sold the fish to the miners. They made much money in this way, and they worked on the farm in the evenings. One evening when Jim was at work on the farm, he saw a sunfish out near Céim so he ran home and told Mike. The two of them ran to the boat and rowed out to the fish and drove the gaff in his eye. It swam out the bay towing the boat after him. They killed the fish near Dursey and sold it in Castletown. They quarrelled over the way the money was divided between them, and Jim killed Mike and threw his body in a cuas, and his ghost is to be seen there on certain times of the year.

Informant: Diarmuid Ó hArrachtáin, aged 88, farmer, Cahermeeleboe, Co. Cork

The Magician and the Miser

Long ago an old woman who lived in the village of Cluin was supposed to be highly skilled in diabolical arts. When cattle got sick, the owner would visit this old woman and obtain a cure from her. She treated everything likewise, and all her cures proved successful. Her fame spread far and wide. One day an old woman visited her. She had been suffering from rheumatism for a number of years and came for a cure. The old woman knew that her visitor was a great miser. She told her she should go to a warm climate, but the miser thought this too expensive. The old woman told her she could give her no cure without money. The miser then went home. Every day she visited the magician but got no cure as she would not pay. The magician knew of the woman's greed for money and her grief in parting with it, so she was plotting some scheme to get rid of her for ever. She knew nobody would feel lonely after her. Next day the miser visited her as usual, little knowing that it would be her last time. The magician told her if she paid her a little sum of money, she would do her best for her. The miser did so very reluctantly. Then the magician told her to go for a long walk to the hill of Gúala, to lift a large boulder there, and underneath it she would find lots of money and when she would arrive home, her rheumatism would be healed after the exercise. This was a trap she had laid for the miser, and the latter was delighted. It was not for the good of her rheumatism she went there but for the money. She set out on her journey in high glee, and within an hour she had the boulder in Gúala hill overturned. She saw all the money and was busily collecting it when the boulder slipped back in its place and trapped her underneath. The people came up to the hill to rescue her, but try as they would, they could not rescue her, so it was decided to let her to her fate as nobody regretted her departure very much. The rock to this day is called Carraigh an Sprúnluightheóra.

Máire Ní Urdail, Cloan, Co. Cork
Informant: Risteárd Ó Duibhir, aged 65, farmer

CLOAN
People, Places and Property

Father Downey

In the penal days there was a boy called John Downey living in Ballydonegan. When the soldiers came here persecuting the catholics he fled to Spain where he was educated and ordained. There was one of the O Sullivan Beares put in his charge as the boy's parents were dead. When the boy grew up, he joined the Spanish army. After a few years in the army, he thought of visiting his native home. But Fr Downey did not want to let him go as he knew the English were watching for all Catholics and that boy was a Catholic, but O Sullivan persisted on going so Fr Downey came with him. They landed in Killmiciloge on the boundary between Cork and Kerry. They went from there on horseback to Finnaha and then they came across Cnoc Fuara to Coom. There they remained hiding from the English soldiers. On Christmas night Fr Downey arranged to have a midnight Mass in Killmiciloge. Two days before Christmas a heavy shower of snow fell over all the surrounding country. On Christmas night the people were stealing away to the house in which Fr Downey was saying the Mass and a man who saw them told Puxley in Dunboy who followed the footprints in the snow to the house in which Fr Downey was saying Mass. They hid in the wood nearby until he was alone with the boy and they then rushed in and killed him. The man who informed on him fell over a cliff in Cnoc an Fiolar and was killed. The eagles ate all his body only leaving his tongue and his hands.

Seantithe na Seanaimsire

Long ago the people of this parish lived in different houses from the houses we have at present. They were low houses with thatched roofs. The walls were made of stone and earth. They mixed the earth with water until it was soft and then they put it on the stones. In some of the houses there were no chimneys, but they had holes in the roof to let the smoke out. The fuel they burned was furze, bushes, roots, brosna and scalps. There were big fireplaces in some of the houses. The houses were lime washed inside and around the door and windows on the outside. There was a settle in every house. It was used as a settle during the day and as a bed during the night. There was a plank on the side and when it was lifted up the settle was like a box. The light the people had long ago was a candle which they made themselves. In the old houses there were cupboards built into the walls.

Collector: Diarmuid Ó hArrachtáin, Cahermeeleboe, Co. Cork
Informant: Diarmuid Ó hArrachtáin, 88 years, farmer

Bóithre An Cheantair

There are names on many of the roads in this parish. There is a road leading from Cahermeelaboe to Cluin called the Company Scout. It is so called because it was made by a mining company. There is another road called the Dairy Road. It is so called because there was a dairy company stationed on a place called the Floors beside the road. This company bought milk from the neighbouring farmers and the milk was brought to the dairy in carts along this road. There is an old road leading to Castletown Bere. It is not used now as there was another road made. There is a track in Cahermore which was used by the people in olden days when they were going to mass. It is called Bóthair An Aifrinn and it is still used as a short cut by the people. There are also many other short cuts in this district. There are many crossroads in the place. There is a crossroad called the Priest's Cross. It is so called as it is near the presbytery. Long ago the people held dances there. There is a crossroad in Reentrisk called Caribal. There is a dance held there every Sunday. There are other crosses called the Ballydonegan Cross, the Killogue Cross, the North Allihies Cross and the South Allihies Cross.

Place Names

The district of Allihies consists of nine townlands. They are Cluin, Ballydonegan, Cahermeelaboe, Coom, Coominches, Allihies, Barness, Fuhir, and Kealogue. The word Cluin means a meadow or low-lying land. Ballydonegan is an Irish word meaning Town of The Donegans. This townland is named after a famous clan called the Donegans who lived there. Cahermeelaboe is also an Irish word meaning City of The Thousand Cows. The word Coom means a hollow as this barony is situated at the foot of a hill in a class of glen. Coominches means green low-lying land divided into two parts by a narrow river. Allihies is so called from the high cliffs which range the seacoast near that district. The word Barness or Bearna means a gap because this district is situated near a class of gap or opening in a hill which separates Allihies from Cahermore. The word Caherine means The Little City. This townland is so called because it is the smallest in this district. The word Fuher is taken from Foithin which means shelter. This townland is situated in a sheltered place.

Collector: Máire Ní Úrdail, Cloan, Co. Cork
Informant: Seán Ó Súilleabháin, aged 68

Names of Fields

These are the names of fields in Cluin. The Buaile is so called because the cows are milked in it. It is in Timothy Kelly's farm. Pairc na Driseoga is so called because the briars grow plentifully in it. It is also the property of Tim Kelly. The Sawmill field is so called because there was a sawmill there long ago. It is on the farm of Jonathan Hodges. Pairc an Sean Tige is so called because there is the ruin of an old house in it. It belongs to Tim Kelly. Pairc Fada is so called as it is a very long field.

Máire Ní Urdail, Cloan, Co. Cork
Informant: Risteárd Ó Duibhir, aged 65, farmer

CLOAN
Farming, Trade and Crafts

Na Prátaí

The farmers in this district sow potatoes once a year, that is in March. At first manure is spread on the field which is about to be tilled or put on the ridges after being ploughed. Sometimes seaweed is put on the bán also. Sand is usually drawn from the strand and also put on the ridges. When the farmer is ready to plough the field, he gets one of his neighbour's horses and his own and ploughs the field into ridges, that is four sods standing together. The old people say that it is not right to leave a ridge without ploughing or setting; síol dearmhad it is called. When the ploughing is completed, he turns the ends of the ridges which are called headlands, with a spade. He then settles them with a spade or a grafán.

It is the woman of the house that usually cuts the scillans. She always takes good care that there is an eye in each one. If the weather was bad and if the scillans could not be sown, they would remain good if they were put into sand. When they are about to sow the scillans small bags are made called scillan bags. When they are all sown, the holes are closed with a shovel so that the frost may not get at them.

After six or seven weeks the trenches are ploughed with one horse and a plough. Then the first earth is put up. When the stalks rise over the ground the second earth is put up. In the month of July, they dig the potatoes. The big potatoes are put in one place called a pit and the small ones, which are called criocans, are put by themselves or into bags and boiled for pigs. The big potatoes are put aside and kept for eating purposes. Then they are covered in straw. There they are left until the end of the year, and they are stored in an outhouse.

Long, long ago the olden people used to make bread out of the potatoes. They used to make two kinds of bread, one was called potato cake and the other one was called stampie cake.

This is how a stampie cake is made. At first a clean piece of tin in which holes are is got. This is called a scraper.

Then unboiled potatoes are scraped into some vessel. After being scraped they are put into a clean cloth and the water taken out of them. Then they are mixed with a little flour just as would be done with any other cake. In the case of care of a potato cake it is how they are boiled at first, and then the cake is made with them. The people long ago used to make a number of those cakes. They used use potatoes and milk for almost every meal.

When the farmer is sowing the potatoes, and when he is finishing the last ridge, he makes it very straight because the old people say that if the last ridge would not be straightened potatoes would not grow in it. If the farmer was ploughing a field in which a líos would be, he would not plough the líos at all. Long ago a man was ploughing a field. There was a líos in the field, so he ploughed the líos also. On the following morning when this man went to the field so as to finish the remainder, the patch which he was after ploughing was turned back again. So, he never ploughed it ever since.

Collector: Máire Ní Murchadha, Allihies, Co. Cork
Informant: Seán Ó Murchadha, 85 years, farmer

CLOAN
Local Customs

Old Customs

The old people had many old customs. These are the ones which I know.

If a person got a haircut, it is right to put the hair into a hole, because when the person dies, he will come back for the hair.

Fishermen do not go fishing on St Bartholomew's night because the old people say that anyone who goes out fishing on that night gets drowned.

If a person got burned it is good to rub a tongue of a fox to it.

If a dog bit a person it would get better if the dog licked the cut three times.

If a knife fell on the ground a gentleman would visit the house and if a fork fell on the ground a lady would visit the house.

If a person got a hairpin on the road, the first one he or she would meet they would marry.

If sparks flew out of a fire, some money would come into that house.

If a person was going on a journey and if a funeral was passing, that person should go along with the funeral until he or she would reach the first cross.

Long ago all the people used to make a potato cake on Michaelmas Day.

If a sod of turf fell out of the fire, a stranger would visit the house.

If a person came into a house to light his pipe when a churn would be making he would not be allowed to do so.

It is a custom to bring in something green from the fields before the sun rises on May Day Morning.

If a person came in, he or she should go out the same door as they came in.

If a person got eggs or a hen to hatch, a pin or penny would be given to the person who gave them.

When eggs are hatched a cross is put on each egg with a burnt stick.

It is not right to put a stick on your shoulder inside a house.

It is not right to open an umbrella inside a house.

If a person's nose was itchy, someone would be talking about him or her.

If a person's right eye was itchy, he or she would be laughing and if the left eye was itchy he or she would be crying.

If a person's ear was ringing like a bell he or she would pray for the dead.

If a person met a foxy cat on the road he or she would have bad luck and if a person met a black cat he would have good luck.

If a person met one magpie on the road it would be for sorrow, two for joy, three for a wedding, four to die, five for silver, six for gold, and seven for a story that was never told. If a person heard the cuckoo with his or her right ear, it would be for good luck. If a person died the clock should be stopped. If a person pulled a tooth, he or she would throw it over the head three times.

Collector: Máire Ní Murchadha, Allihies, Co. Cork
Informant: Seán Ó Murchadha, 85 years, farmer

Féilí na Bliana

On St Stephen's Day the boys dress up in old clothes and put masks on their faces. Then they get a holly bush, ivy and a bunch of ribbons. They get a wren if they can, and if they cannot, they get a hen's head. They tie the holly and ivy to a long pole with the ribbons and fix the wren or the hen's head to the holly. They go around the countryside singing this song.

The wren, the wren the king of all birds
Tis Stephens Day he was caught in the furze
Though the man was little his honour was great.
Stir up my brave landlord and give us a treat.
This landlord is a wealthy man
Into his house I carried my wren
And this little box I bring under my arm
Five or six pennies will do it no harm
So up with the kettle and down with the tea
Give us our money and leave us go away

The people wear shamrock on St Patrick's Day. They eat a lot of pancakes on Shrove Tuesday evening. It is a custom to get married during Shrove. On Ash Wednesday the people put holy ashes on their foreheads. On Good Friday people go to the strand for bairneacs. It is a custom on Easter Sunday to eat as many eggs as possible. On May Day, furze for good luck, bringing in the summer it is called. The people will not sell milk or butter on that day. On St John's night the people light bonfires and drive the cows past them. On the Feast of the Assumption there are sports held in Allihies. On November's night the young people have great fun. They get a bag of apples and a tub of water. They put some of the apples into the tub and try to get them out with their mouths. On New Year's Eve at twelve o'clock the Allihies fife and drum band plays the National Anthem.

Collector: Diarmuid Ó hArrachtáin, Cahermeeleboe, Co. Cork
Informant: Diarmuid Ó hArrachtáin, 88 years, farmer

Local Maritime Phrases and Words

Cuas is a word used by the fishermen of this Parish. A Cuas is a narrow inlet among the rocks through which the Sea runs.

A móirín is a small fish, which is found in rock-pools when the sea goes out.

A Cuilg is a small fish found in shallow water.

Gas is a sea weed which grows on rocks or on the roots of stronger weeds. It's picked and when dried it is eaten. It is brown in colour.

A craoban is a small fish found in rock-pools. It is useless as food.

Barrthaois is a white substance seen in the sea on very dark nights.

Caise is the white foam that the sea makes when it dashes against the rocks.

This is a great place for fishing pollock and conner and bream.

Beal Tuileis the second oar from the bow of the boat on the left side.

Builg is a submerged rock.

Collector: Liam Ó hArrachtáin, Cahermeeleboe, Co. Cork
Informant: Diarmuid Ó hArrachtáin, aged 88, farmer

CLOAN
Local Cures

Leighiseanna

These are the cures the people had in olden times when any disease would be in a person. If a person had a sore mouth, which is called Craos Galar, a gander would be got and if the gander would breathe into the person's mouth three times, the person would get better. If a person was bitten by a dog, it would be good to make the dog lick the cut. If a thorn was on a person's hand or foot, and if the hand or foot got swollen and got bad, it would get better if a fox's tongue would be rubbed to it. If a person was subject to headaches, it would get better if the water that would be crossing a road or any other place in which people cross, would be rubbed to his or her head and make the sign of the cross on the forehead with the water also. If a person cut his or her finger, it would stop bleeding if a cobweb would be put to the wound, or the white part of an unboiled egg. If a person had toothache and if he or she rubbed soot to them it would stop the pain. If a cow was sick, she would get better if she got a bottle of salt-water from the sea. If a cow had some other kind of a disease she would improve if a stick of weeds would be put back her mouth to her throat and taken out again. If a person sprained his or her hand or leg, it would get better if a strip of cloth would be soaked in strong pickle and then tightly around the effected part. If a person had boils, they would get better if dock-leaves would be rubbed to the burned patch. If a person's hand would be stiff, it would get better if palm oil would be rubbed to it. If a person would be suffering from rheumatism it would get better if boiled seaweed called feamnach would be rubbed to the effected part.

The old people say that iron water, that is rusty coloured water, which is to be found only in some places, is very good for a sick person to drink it. If a person had corns, they would get better if he or she would go out on May Day morning before the sun would rise and walk on the dew. If a person had measles, it would be good to get nettles and boil them and drink the water after being boiled. If a person fell and if a lump came on the person's head, it would get better if a penny would be put on the lump. If a person had a burn, it would heal if seal-oil would be rubbed to the burn, or if soda would be put to it and a white cloth tightly put around the burned patch.

Collector: Máire Ní Murchadha, Allihies, Co. Cork
Informant: Seán Ó Murchadha, 85 years, farmer

CLOAN
Natural World and Weather Lore

Ainmhithe Allta

These are the wild animals which are in this district. The rabbit, the hare, the badger, the fox, the weasel, and the otter. The rabbit is the most common of all the animals. This district is infested with them. Everywhere a person would travel, the rabbits are to be seen. The rabbits in this parish do great damage to the farmers. A few years ago, there was such a vast number of them in the district that the farmers who kept five or six cows could only keep one. All the fields are full of burrows and worse still the animals cannot eat the grass which the rabbit's taste. This year the rabbits are not plentiful as they were in past years because the farmers employed trappers this year. Those trappers killed a huge number of them. Some of them went to the hills and it is supposed that before long they will be as thick as ever. Rabbits live on grass and clover.

Hares are not as plentiful as the rabbits. The hares in this district are not as swift and as good for running as the hares in other parts of the country. It is very easy to catch the hares in this parish. Hares are very harmless, they usually feed on carrots.

The fox is a very common animal also and is known as a very clever animal. The fox lives in a den. The fox does great harm to the farmer's wife in the line of killing hens and ducks. The fox is very clever. Once a very cute fox came to a neighbour's duck house. In the morning the farmer went out and could not find his ducks. He was thinking that it was Mr Fox that killed them. A few days afterwards the farmer was walking near a tillage field and he heard a duck noising. He looked around and to his great surprise he saw a duck's head over the earth. It was the clever fox who couldn't eat them all, covered one of them in the earth and left its head up so that he could know where he left it.

The following story shows the cleverness of a fox. Long, long ago a man from Dursey Island went to Kenmare by boat. While he was there, he killed a fox and brought him to the island. When he took the fox out of the boat it was alive as it ran away. The fox then made a den at the edge of a cliff. Until that time there was not one single fox in the island. This fox started to kill all the hens and ducks. They could not kill him in any way. He used always go to the den in the cliff so the dogs could not get at him. There was a briar going from the top of the cliff down to the den. The people thought of a plan which was to cut the briar, and they did so. While the fox was out one day, they put the dogs after him. The fox made for his den but as soon as he put his foot on the briar, he found it broken. He fell down into the deep sea and got drowned.

Collector: Máire Ní Murchadha, Allihies, Co. Cork
Informant: Seán Ó Murchadha, 85 years, farmer

An Doineann

Storms rage frequently in this locality owing to its bleak position near the Atlantic Ocean. Sometimes a land storm takes place, other times it is a sea storm and very often both take place at the same time. A fearful storm raged through the neighbourhood about nine years ago. This storm prevailed during the festival of Christmas, and it was not a very happy one for the people as they were in dread of the gale. Many houses were broken, and a few were left almost roofless. Hay sheds were knocked and over-turned. Many tombstones were knocked in the local cemeteries, and a number of other damages were also caused. A crew of fishermen went out fishing in a seine boat in a place called Tráigh An Phéarla about two miles from this district. The fishermen left the coast early in the evening. They were not gone very far when signs of a storm appeared. They kept rowing however and after a little while the storm arose. They tried to bring the boat back to the strand, but they did not succeed in doing so. The boat was overturned, and every member of the crew was thrown into the sea and drowned. The boat was completely destroyed, and the tragedy was considered to be one of the most disastrous ever witnessed in the locality.

Collector: Máire Ní Úrdail, Cloan, Co. Cork
Informant: Seán Ó Súilleabháin, aged 68

CLOAN
Sea and Shipwrecks

Crúadhtan

A dreadful calamity occurred on Reentrisk strand on St Bartholomew's Night about eighteen years ago. A crew consisting of about seventeen fishermen left the strand in two boats that evening. One boat was about thirty feet in length and the other about twenty feet. The district of Reentrisk is situated about three miles to the northwest of the village of Cluin. Its coastline is very rugged, and numbers of submerged rocks are very plentiful throughout the harbour. These rocks are called builgs. The fishermen left the coast early in the evening. They fished round the bay for some time and had a good supply of fish. They then rowed homewards to the shore. There were ten men in one boat and the other contained seven. They rowed for some time but when they were almost to the shore, they discovered that a storm was arising. When they reached the vicinity of the builgs the sea was very rough. They did their utmost to gain the shore but while they were trying to do so a huge wave overturned the boat, and the men were cast into the sea and drowned with the exception of one man who still lives in Reentrisk. As a result of that awful tragedy no crew of fishermen ever since went fishing on St Bartholomew's Night.

Collector: Máire Ní Úrdail, Cloan, Co. Cork
Informant: Seán Ó Súilleabháin, aged 68

REENTRUSK

Co. Chorcaighe
Bar: Béara
Par: Cil na Manach
Scoil: Rinn Troisc
Oide: Domhnall Ó Súilleabháin

REENTRUSK
People, Places and Property

Landlords

The names of the landlords were Mr Pain, Mr Hitchen, Mr Turner, and Mr Edles. The landlords were very long in the place. They were very bad landlords. They put the farmers out of their farms and the people went away to foreign countries. The landlords came from England and took the land off the people, and they had to pay a high rent.

Collector: Anna Harrington.
Informant: James Harington, aged 68, Reentrusk, Co. Cork

Gurtahig

The name of my townland is called Gurtahig. The reason why it is called Gurtahig is there were giants there long ago. The meaning of Gurtahig is the Giant's corn field. They were very strong giants. The hurley ball they had was a big rock and ten men could not lift it. It is there always below the road that is going towards Urhan. It is said that one of them jumped from Urhan to Beal and he threw a stone the distance from Garnish to Gurtahig. There was one in Cleinough and one in Urhan. The one in Urhan got a bone of a horse and he threw it into Cleinough and hit the other giant with the bone and broke his head in half.

Collector: Eileen Sullivan
Informant: Patrick Sullivan, aged 66, Reentrusk, Co. Cork

Eskivaude

The townland in which I live is called Eskivaude. It is situated in the parish of Allihies and the barony of Castletownbere. The reason why it was called Eskivaude is because it was there the first boat in Reentrisk was built. There were eight houses there long ago and there are only five houses in it now. The houses that were there were thatched houses. The Sullivans are more numerous than the Harringtons. There are only two people who can speak Irish. There is only one woman who is getting the pension. Her name is Mrs Sullivan and she can tell Irish stories.

Collector: Julia Kelly
Informant: Patrick Leary, Reentrusk, Co. Cork

Houses Long Ago

They used to have thatch, timber and sods as roofs. Very few houses were made of slates. They got thatch on the hill, and they used straw also. There was a bed in the kitchen in some houses. It was placed near the fire. Old used sleep in it. The hearth was in the middle of the gable, and it was made of stone and mortar. The floor was made of earth. There were no chimneys in the houses only a hole in the roof for a chimney. The old people never heard of the fireplace being in the middle of the floor. There was only one door but in some of the houses there were two doors. They had a few iron bolts they found after storms and the others were timber bolts. They had only one window in the kitchen. It was of timber, and it was opened by day and shut by night. There was a half door in every house, long ago. The people used turf roots for fuel. They had small oil lamps placed near the fire. They had candles made from tallow they got from the sea or animals. They made them in a mould. A mould was a piece of iron with a hole in the middle of it, and two holes in the side and a hole in the bottom. They melted the tallow and put it into the mould, and they put timber in the holes so the grease would not come out. When it would harden it would be the shape of candles.

Collector: Mr Dan Kelly, aged 69 Reentrusk, Co. Cork
Informant: Mrs Dan Kelly, aged 70

An Old School

Long ago there was a school in the townland of Boloughacahireen. It was whitewashed outside and inside and there was a slate roof on it. The teacher used to teach the children in the school. The subjects she used to teach to them were reading, writing, arithmetic, history, and geography. They didn't speak Irish in the school because the teacher didn't know it. They had copybooks and writing pens, and they had slate and slate pencils for doing sums. There were six or seven desks in the school. The name of the teacher was Miss Regan, and she was a very learned teacher.

Collector: Julianna Harrington
Informant: Mrs Michael Sullivan, aged 72, Reentrusk, Co. Cork

REENTRUSK
Farming, Trade and Crafts

Buying and Selling

Shops were plentiful long ago. There were two shops in Reentrisk and one in Barnes. There were shops also in Cluin. The people bought their goods in those shops. Articles were not sold near the church. Money was plentiful long ago. It was money they gave for goods long ago. They did not work for goods. There was not any bad luck on any particular day, but it was said that things you buy from a deceitful shopkeeper were unlucky. They sold things on Sundays also.

Long ago they salted the butter and put it into firkins and brought it to Cork. Porter was sold a tuppence a pint and an ounce of tobacco at threepence long ago. The people sold oats, straw and potatoes. Pedlars came around the place. They sold clothes and tea. They had side cars coming around. The pedlars used not buy anything from the people.

Collector: Mr Dan Kelly, aged 69 Reentrusk, Co. Cork
Informant: Mrs Dan Kelly, aged 74

Shops

There were three shops in this parish long ago. The people used buy their goods in those shops and in Castletown. There weren't any goods sold near the Church after mass. Money was plentiful long ago. The people bought their goods for money. Goods were exchanged long ago. The people gave a day's work for goods also. It was unlucky to buy a new garment or to dwell in a new house on New Year's Day, Good Friday or in Lent. They sold their butter in Castletown or in Cork. They sold fish and potatoes and other crops. Pedlars came around the place long ago, they sold clothes, tea, pins and needles. They bought rags, irons, copper bolts and horsehair from the people.

Informant: James Harrington, aged 68, Reentrusk, Co. Cork

Trades

There were more tramps going through the country long ago than what are going around now. There were not any candle-makers in this district. Soap wasn't made here either. There was a basket maker in this place. His name was Michael Leary. He lived in Cleinough. He used grow rods in his farm. There was a smith here also. He lived in Eskinane and his name was Dan Sullivan. There were no weavers or painters in this place. The Danes used to tan leather. The people used to make ropes of hay and straw. They used to have a crúisín. There was a thatcher in this place named Daniel Harrington. There was not any churn, wheel or nail maker in this district.

Informant: James Harrington, aged 68, Reentrusk, Co. Cork

Candlemakers

There were candlemakers in Reentrisk. They got the tallow from the sea and made candles. There were no soap makers or weavers or ropemakers in the district. There was a basket maker in Cleinough and a smith in Eskinane. There was a churn maker in Gurtahig his name was Taidhg Ó Dheí. Ceardaí beag blasta ní do dhéanach geacht ní gaibh agus cara h -imsta tamall tar éis báis [A nice little handy carpenter for making everything for the people and coffins to stretch a while after dying].

Informant: Patrick Sullivan, aged 66

Clothes

There are seven tailors in this parish. Long ago they used to go from house to house making clothes. They don't keep any clothes in their houses and used not long ago. They make the clothes in their own houses now. Long ago the tailors had not any machines. The tailors used to make shirts in the houses. They were made of wool. The wool was dyed and spun. They knit some of their own stockings, but they don't sell any. Long ago they spun wool and dyed it and made stockings of it. Thread is got in the shops now. Black clothes are worn after a person's death now.

Collector: Mr Dan Kelly, aged 69 Reentrusk, Co. Cork
Informant: Mrs Dan Kelly, aged 74

Boots

The people were twenty years before they wore shoes long ago. Some old did not ever wear shoes. The children go bare footed now all the year round. It is not right to throw out the feet water. It is said it would be thrown back up on you again. It is not right to have two feet waters in the house at night. It is said you should bring in clean water before you throw out the feet water.

John Murphy repaired shoes. There was a shoemaker in Eskivaude. His name was Denis Cullen. My grandfather in Eskinane wore shoes with timber soles. They were made in Cork. There was leather canned in this place when the Danes were here.

Informant: James Harrington, aged 68, Reentrusk, Co. Cork

Potatoes

Potatoes are planted every year. Manure from the cowhouses is spread over the ground first. Then it is turned by means of spades. The men of the house usually do this and where there is only one man in the house a neighbour helps. Ploughs are not used, the farms being small, and there are scarcely any horses. The ground is turned into ridges by spades bought in the shops. Potatoes are cut into skillauns. There is only one eye left in each skillaun. The skillauns are left in the house for a few days. They are put into a skillaun bag i.e. a little bag tied around the waist and the sower sticks the spade in the ridge, then throws a skillaun into the hole made by the spade. The skillauns are planted about nine inches apart. The holes are then closed by striking them with a spade. After a few weeks the ridges are earthed. Sometimes the ridges are manured when this is not already done before they are turned. When the plants are over the ground the ridges are second earthed. They are sprayed about the month of June and if the weather is wet they are sprayed again about a month later. They are dug in September or October by means of spades. They are then put into pits. The pits are made by levelling a bit of ground and placing the potatoes on it. They are then covered with grass or rushes and after a few weeks this is covered with earth. Kinds of potatoes include Champions, Epicures, Aran Banners, Kerr Pinks, and Irish Queens.

REENTRUSK
Local Customs

St Stephen's Day

The young boys go in the wren, and they put old clothes on them so the people would not know them. They get sticks and put papers and rags on the sticks and they go to every house in Reentrisk for money, and they sing songs. On St Patrick's Day the people wear badges. People get married in Shrove. The people fast in Lent. It is said it is not right to throw out the ashes on Ash Wednesday. People bring in something green Mayday. They say that's bringing in the summer. People light bushes near the gardens on St John's Day. Long ago Michaelmas Day was a great day paying rounds.

Informant: Patrick Leary, aged 74

Food

Long ago they used eat four meals a day, namely breakfast, dinner, an evening meal, and supper. They used eat their breakfast at nine o' clock, dinner at two o'clock, tea at four, and supper at eight o'clock. They worked three or four hours before breakfast. They used eat potatoes for breakfast and bread and milk sometimes. They used drink a lot of milk. The table used be placed near the wall. The kinds of bread they used to eat is boxty, stampy, wheaten bread, and meal bread. Boxty was made from potatoes, wheaten flour milk and butter. They used to make stampy from grated potatoes, squeezed in a piece of cloth and it was baked. Some people killed a cow for meat. They used eat a lot of fish such as mackerel, herring, ling, cod, hake and congers.

Collector: Mr Dan Kelly, aged 69 Reentrusk, Co. Cork
Informant: Mrs Dan Kelly, aged 74

The Feast of the Year

On St Stephen's Day a gathering of grown-up boys dress up in old clothes and get a pole, holly, ivy, and a wren. They go to every house they sing and dance and play. On St Patrick's Day they burn a piece of timber and when it cools, they make they sign of the cross on their right hand. They say it is not right to spill milk or throw out ashes on Ash Wednesday or May Day. They used not drink milk or eat eggs or butter and they used fast on Good Friday. They used to bring in bornacs or feóil fairrge they called them. On Palm Sunday palms are blessed and distributed. On Easter Sunday each person eats three or four eggs. On the first of May the people bring in furze, holly and ivy and flowers, bringing in the Summer. St John's day, the twenty fourth of June, bushes are lit near the cows, the meadow and the garden. Michaelmas Day was a great day long ago eating apples. The people of this parish go to a pattern making rounds. Oidhche Pártlán is a night held by the fishermen in memory of the five men that got drowned fifteen years last August. The fishermen don't go out that night. It falls on the twenty-third of August each year. In this place they celebrate Christmas night on the night of the twenty fourth.

Collector: Mr Dan Kelly, aged 69 Reentrusk, Co. Cork
Informant: Mrs Dan Kelly, aged 74

Holy Wells

There is a holy well in the townland of Eskininane, Reentrisk. Rounds were paid there years ago, and people still pay them there. The well is in the lands of Patrick Downey, Eskininane. People throw in stones while paying rounds there and also when passing by. Rounds are paid on any Saturday evening after the sun goes down and again on Sunday morning before the Sun rises. The person walks around the well and while doing so says one Our Father and ten Hail Marys, then he throws in a stone. This is done nine times. The same thing is done on the following morning. The well is beside a rock and is almost full of stones. There is very little water in it. There is no tree nearby. It is believed that if anyone would take anything out, he would get sick.

Informant: Patrick Downey, aged 73, Eskininane, Co. Cork,

REENTRUSK
Local Cures

Cures

This is how measles is cured. People get boiled churn milk that is two weeks old to drink. Toothache is cured by leaving a churn for two weeks without washing and get the snoss that grows on it and put it on the tooth. It is also cured by putting bread soda into the tooth.

Collector: Michael Sullivan
Informant: Daniel Sullivan, aged 76, Reentrusk, Co. Cork

Ringworm: They used to put a rim of ink around the sore.
Warts: They used get a rotten potato or the water of potatoes and rub it to the warts.
Sores: They mix soap and sugar and warm it and put it on the sore to cure it. They boil white bread in a cup of boiling water and squeeze it and put it on a bruise to make a drop. Dock leaf is put on sores also.
Boils: They used bath them with hot water and put dock leaf on them or linseed meal.
Toothache: To rub soda or salt or whiskey to the tooth.
Colds: To drink plenty whey, milk and medicine.

Collector: Mr Dan Kelly, aged 69 Reentrusk, Co. Cork
Informant: Mrs Dan Kelly, aged 74

REENTRUSK
Natural World and Weather Lore

Storms

The only storm the old people remember was the storm in the year when the Calf Rock lighthouse was wrecked. It was on the Calf Rock the lighthouse was then. A man named Michael O'Shea was an uncle to Jim Harrington in Coomeen. He rescued the lightkeepers who had been weather bound for nine days. The storm came in and several boats were wrecked. It came up as far as the bridge in Tranferla. It also came up near John Sullivan's house. It covered many fields by the sea and destroyed crops. When the storm was over, the places on which it covered there were a lot of fish left, especially pikey-dogs and congers. In the year of the big wind, eighteen thirty-nine, many houses' roofs and stacks were knocked. There were several signs of the storm such as the blue light in the fire and the curlews were crying around the houses.

Collector: Mr Dan Kelly, aged 69 Reentrusk, Co. Cork
Informant: Mrs Dan Kelly, aged 74

Southern Reporter and Cork Commercial Courier

Tuesday 8 January 1839

Great Storm on Sunday Night

We were visited on Sunday night with one of the most tremendous gales of wind every remembered here. It commenced to blow hard at 8 o'clock, from W.S.W., but at half-past 11 the storm assumed a strength and fury almost irresistible, and continued with unabated violence until 6 o'clock on Monday morning, when it considerably lulled. As might naturally be looked for, extensive damage, by the falling in of chimneys and unroofing of houses, has been experienced. The gable end of a house in Caroline-street gave way, and has caused much mischief to the houses adjoining. Scores of chimneys fell – some through roofs, and others into the streets. The largest and stoutest trees have been torn up by the roots; but that which best attests to the uncontrollable force of the gale is to be found in the prostration of between 30 and 40 feet of the balustrades of the western side of Patrick's Bridge. This casualty occurred at about 12 o'clock. Several persons were passing at the moment, each, with difficulty, keeping his feet, and one gentleman had just disengaged his grasp of one of the battlement stones, when, to the extend stated, the bridge gave way, and some four or five tonnes of solid mason work and eight or ten thick columns, fell to the ground with a loud and heavy crush.

REENTRUSK
Sea and Shipwrecks

Cistí Óir i bhFolach

According to local tradition, a ship came in and got wrecked at Tranferla, a townland in this district. The name of the ship was The Pearl. Hence the strand got the name of Tranferla and the district near it got the same name. The ship carried gold. The sailors carried this to a field nearby where they hid it. The place is now called Esc an Airgid. The money was buried when the moon was shining, and a patch of moonlight or shadow was the only mark they had. When the moon went down the sailors came back to get the gold but could not find it. Some men searched the place about fifty years ago but without success.

REENTRUSK
History and Archaeology

The Famine

The Famine effected this place very much. Almost half the people died. There were three times more people in Reentrisk at the time of the famine than are there now. Some of the women and children went away through the country asking alms and they died along the roads. The people died all over the country. Many of them died around here. Very few lived. The people ate grass nettles and animals. This was how the famine came on. One night a plague of frost and gale came and burned the stalks. The plants were growing up after being second earthed when they rotted. The people got foreign seed the next year from the English Government. The potatoes were planted in ridges as they are now. They made stampy of bad black potatoes. The people had bornacs, tropaun and carrigeen moss instead of the potatoes. They did not get any assistance or grants that year. Most of the people died of hunger. Food was not scarce since the time of the famine.

Collector: Mr Dan Kelly, aged 69 Reentrusk, Co. Cork
Informant: Mrs Dan Kelly, aged 74

Líoses

There is a líos in the townland of Coomeen. It is a round small rock. There is not any hole in the rock. The Danes had not anything to do with this líos. When people used be milking they heard the fairies crying. There are many stories told about it. Long ago a woman was spreading seaweed in a field near the líos. She was hit with a sod. It was about seven o'clock in the evening. There is a light every night in winter around the líos. There is a cuas near the líos. A small sailing ship was lost there. There are many other stories told about it.

Informant: James Harington, aged 70, Coonan, Co. Cork

There is a líos near John Sullivan's in Boloughacahireen. The name of the líos is the Fairy Líos. The shape of the líos is a round hole. It is said that it was the fairies made it. The fairies lived on it. Wild cats and animals are seen there. There were lights seen near it. People often heard music and dancing in the líos.

Collector: Julia Kelly
Informant: Patrick Leary, aged 74, Reentrusk, Co. Cork

URHAN

Co. Chorcaighe
Bar: Béara
Par: Cill Chaitiairn
Scoil: Urhan (B & C)
Oide: Seán Ó Murchadha (Urhan B)
Eimile Ní Urdail (Urhan C)

URHAN
Local Folklore and Stories

Loch a'Quinnleáin

Long ago there was an Irish priest in Germany. One day he met a woman. This woman was from the north of Germany, and she was telling him about Loch a'Quinnleáin but he did not understand her. She said that there was a lake in the north of Germany and the people used to pay visits there on the 8th of July every year. This priest was a parish priest and sometime afterwards he came to the parish of Tuosist in Lauragh, he did not know anything about Loch a'Quinnleáin then. He was not long in Lauragh when the time came that the people used to pay the visits to Loch a'Quinleáin on the 7th and 8th of July. It was then he thought of what the German woman had told him.

There are three banks in the lake now. Long ago these banks were near the lake, and it is said that these banks used to move. So, at last they were seen going into the lake. Every morning they used to stir and if they would stir when a person would be making the rounds it was a sure sign of a cure. Sometimes when the banks used to move, they used to go in a line across the lake or on to each other in the middle of the lake. There was a saileach tree growing out of one of the banks and it is said that it withered many years ago, but it never died out or never got green again. It is to be seen there still.

It is said that long ago the people used to see three soft sods rising out from one of the banks. These three sods were somewhat like the shape of a duck, legs and all, and the last sod used to be lame. The people used call these three sods the triopols. When the three sods would rise out, they would turn to the left side of the bank and go all around near the edge of the lake once and then back to the bank and go in the same hole again.

Collector: Pádruig Ó Síothcháin, Caherkeen, Co. Cork
Informant: Máire Ní Shíothcháin, Grandparent

Loch a' quinnleáin is situated in Lauragh. It is connected with St Quinlann. People go there from all parts of the country for the good of their health. They perform rounds there. The rounds are performed by going around a bank where it is said that St Quinlan was buried. People go there three times during life. There are three little lakes quite close to the bank where the people finish their rounds, then they take a drink of the water.

Collector: Domnall Ó Súilleabháin, Eyeries, Co. Cork

The Ghostly Hurlers

Long ago there was a priest and a layman travelling together on a fine summer's evening. The layman was a friend of the priest. As they were going along the valley the priest was looking towards the high ground at the foot of the mountain. He asked the layman if he saw anything, and the layman said he did not. Then the priest told him to look at such a place to see if he could then see anything. Then the man asked the priest what did he see and he told him that he saw a great multitude of people armed with hurleys as if they were playing. Then the priest told him to move more closer to him, but he could not see. At last, he told him to stand right back of him nearly in his footsteps. The man did as he was told and then he saw the great multitude of people and they appeared to be happy.

John Cornelius Mic Daniel O'Sullivan

Long ago there lived a man whose name was John Cornelius Mic Daniel O'Sullivan. He lived during the time of the famine. He had ten children and four of them died. He got a job on the road going to town and his pay was fourpence a day. One morning he got up very early to go to Eyeries for bread for his breakfast but when he reached Eyeries all the bread was sold out. When he found that he could not get any bread he went away working in the road, and he had no dinner that day or no supper. When he came home in the evening his wife sent him to Eyeries again. He went to Eyeries on horseback, but he found out that there was no bread there. Then he went to town, he had a cousin in town, and he went into her house, and he asked for a bit of bread. She had the contract for the workhouse, and she said she had only ten loaves for the breakfast in the morning, he said to her that he would give her a half a crown for a quarter of a loaf, he said that if she would not give him a piece of bread, he and his family would be dead before morning. So, she gave him a quarter of a loaf. Then he ran out to his horse and jumped on her back and went home as fast as he could, so that he would give them a bit of bread to keep them alive. The bridle he had was the hair of the horse's and the cow's tails traced.

Collector: Seán Ó Súilleabháin, Coulagh, Co. Cork

Comhla bhreac

There is a comhla bhreac in Bill Harrington's hill. Long ago there was a man from Coulagh cutting turf near the comhla bhreac and he saw a ship fully rigged leaving the comla breac. It sailed through the sliabh through Díseart and disappeared. Once there was a man after sheep. He stood on top of the comhla bhreac. He heard the noise under him, he did not know what it was so he ran as quickly as he could. When he was a distance from the rock he looked back. The rock was opened out, and he heard the noise of horses' hoofs and music.

Collector: Seán Ó Súilleabháin, Coulagh, Co. Cork

There is a chomhla bhreac in Tráigh Mhara near Jim Downing's shed. One night long ago, when the fishermen were fishing, they heard the noise. It was like two hills falling against each other. There are two stones standing there. The place was haunted. One night the fishermen were resting there, eating their lunch. There were barrels outside the shed, one barrel was taken off the ground and it rested in the same place again.

Collector: Peadar Ó hÚrdail, Eyeries, Co. Cork

There was a man in Cahirkeem long ago and he never believed in ghosts. One day he was going to the hill and when he was going west, he saw a ghost driving a cow into a big black rock, and when the ghost came to the rock he disappeared. The rock is now called the comhla bhreac. The man got so frightened that he never went to the hill anymore until he died.

Collector: Seán Ó Ceallaigh, Caherkeen, Co. Cork

A Ghost Story

Long ago there lived a shoemaker and he had one son. This son did not care about his trade. He used be out every night gambling and playing cards, and he used come home at late hours. His father used to scold him. One night after this boy coming home his father told him he would see fairies yet. He asked his father where were they. His father told him to go out the next night at twelve o'clock in the big field near the house and to stop at the gate and he would see the biggest sight he had ever seen. The boy said, "very well." Twelve o'clock came the next night and he stayed at the gate and there he saw the crowd coming on. The first man that came to the gate struck a football a kick, then all the crowd followed on. They played on the game and after a while, they made a team on both sides, and while the match was going on one of them got hurt. He came up to where this boy was watching on. And the boy asked him if he was hurt. He said yes. The boy said he would take his place, throwing his coat off. They played the match on and won the game on the side where this boy was. They put on their coats again and walked away and he followed them until they came to a house. They went in and there were tables laid before them, with all kinds of food. They all took their chairs and sat down, except this boy who had none. He asked his partner to give half the chair to sit on and he said yes. But he had no fork. He asked his partner for the fork, and he said yes. When they all got through eating, they got ready to go to bed. Each man had a single bed, but he had none, he asked his partner would he give him part of his bed to sleep, he said yes. He went to bed and when he woke in the morning he was still at the gate

Collector: Eibhlin Ní Suileabhain, Caherkeen, Co. Cork
Informant: Seamus Ó Aractain, aged 60, farmer

An Cailleach Bhéara

The Cailleach Bhéara lived long ago in the mines. She was a very wicked woman. It is said that she flew from the mines to Coulagh and from Coulagh to Kilcatherine. There was a monastery in Cill na Manach. A monk from Cill na Manach followed her. He turned her into a stone in Kilcatherine. The print of her foot is on a rock in Coulagh. There is a rock in Kilcatherine and it is supposed to be her. It is supposed she had a big crab on her door. If anyone should come to the door the crab would catch him and keep him there.

Collector: Seán Ó Néill, Coulagh, Co. Cork
Informant: Bríghid Ní Néill, Grandmother

It is hundreds and hundreds of years since the people of Coulagh heard of this so called bird which they think came down from the mountains and rested on a rock on Coulagh for one night and then went to Kilcatherine. The print of her foot is on the rock yet and will be for ever. The water that rests on the spot will cure warts and it will never dry. The bird is the shape of a woman and she has a basket on her back and the old people say that it is a basket of eggs.

Collector: Proinnséas Ní Néill, Coulagh, Co. Cork
Informant: Concubar Ó Néill, aged 66

Máire Ní Mhurchadha

Máire Ní Mhurchadha lived in Eyeries. Anything that was to happen she used to foretell it. The fairies used to come every night to her house. There is a rock in Béal na Leaptha called the comhla bhreac. It is the shape of a door. One day Máire was coming from town behind a man on a horse. When they reached the top of Béal na Leaptha she came off the horse and told the man to stay there until she would come back. She went towards the rock and the man followed her. She turned back and said he had no right to interfere. They both came back to Eyeries. She was very angry with him and told him that she should travel all the ways to another comhla bhreac in Kerry that night to get information that he interrupted. The man came back to Cahirckeem. There was a parish priest in Eyeries. His name was Fr O'Reilly. One night he was over to Kilcatherine on a sick call. When he was coming home, he fell off the horse and he was hurt. He went into a house and the woman bandaged him. The next Sunday he had a sermon from the altar about Máire Ní Mhurcada. When she heard it, she was mad. She asked did he remember the night that he was coming home from Kilcatherine and only for herself he would be killed.

Collector: Shéosamh Ó Mhurchadha, Caherkeen, Co. Cork

Long ago there lived in Eyeries a woman name Máire Ní Mhurchadha. She was a wise woman. She would tell what would be going to happen to you. She used always be with the fairies. One night a man was coming from the Mines. It was very late, and he was taken away by the fairies. They had a hurley match in the Slieve of Allihies and Máire Ní Mhurchadha was with them. She told this man if they would be giving him anything to eat not to take it, or if he would he should stay with them. The fairies were trying to keep him but Máire Ní Mhurchadha told them not to keep him because his father had not anyone but him. Then they left the man go home to his father. After going home, he got sick, and they asked him where he was all night, and he did not tell them. Máire Ní Mhurchadha heard he was sick and she went to the house and told them to get a Mass said for him that he was in the fairies. Then his father went to the Priest and told him to say Mass for his son. Then the Priest said Mass for the man and after some time the man got better.

Collector: Cáit Ní Dhomhnuidhe, Urhin, Co. Cork
Informant: Miceál O Dhomhnuidhe, father, aged 55, farmer

Máire Ní Mhurchadha lived in Eyeries. There was a Parish Priest in Eyeries named Fr O'Reilly and he used be all the time talking about her, and trying to banish her. One night he was coming from Ardgroom and near the bridge of Bawrs his hat was taken off him. He came off the horse and went trying for it and he could not get it. In the end he got it. When Máire Ní Mhurchadha met him some days after she asked him why was he talking about her, and did he remember the night that he was coming from Ardgroom that his hat fell off. She said only for herself he would be trying for it until morning, and he would not get it. The priest never spoke of Máire Ní Murchadha afterwards. Máire Ní Mhurchadha saved lots of people. There was a boy working in the Mines once and Máire Ní Mhurchadha told him if he would go working there the next day it would be his last day there, and some other boy went in his place, and he got killed.

Collector: Siobhán Ní Mhurchadha, Caherkeen, Co. Cork
Informant: Seán Ó Mhurchadha, father, aged 50, farmer

There was a man living in Gour long ago. He was very ill, and he told someone to send for Máire Ní Mhurchadha. This was a woman that was living in Eyeries Beg. It was said that when she was young, she was brought away in the fairies and she stayed in them. She had the power to work charms. When she came to the man that was dying, she told him that his cure was in his father's grave. She said to get the strongest man around that would go with her into the grave. They got John Hanley from Urhan and they went to the grave about midnight. When she was working the charm, something came against her, and she told the man to take her out of the grave. He took her on his lap and took her down to some stable in Castletown. She stayed there until bright day. She was vomiting through the night. The dying man got better, for it was she that suffered his share. That is about eighty years ago.

One fine summer evening, a man in Caherkeem ate his supper and after eating he went out without any cap on his head. There were six men from the other world coming up the road towards his own house and Máire Ní Murchadha with them. They were going for a woman in this parish who had a baby. When they saw this man Máire Ní Mhurchadha said that that man would do, and they said alright. After a while they disappeared and when the men went in home, he fell dead on the floor.

Long ago there lived in Coulagh a woman who was going to have a wedding party. One day the woman got her horse and basket and went away for the wedding goods. When she went home, she went to bed and when she woke up after a sleep, she felt a great pain in her hip. So, she started to scream and shout with pain. Máire Ní Mhurchadha lived in Eyeries beag at that time. There were very few doctors that time. The woman said to send for Máire Ní Mhurchadha When Máire came she said to the woman, that she came out lucky that she did not get killed last night. Máire looked at the woman's hip and said that she would get a cure from one of her neighbours. The woman told her story to Máire Ní Mhurchadha, she said that when she was coming home, she saw a foxy woman walking beside the horse. She said that her horse was sulking and that she started to beat her horse and pull her wherever she wanted to. Once she pulled the horse across the road and one of the baskets went fast to the foxy woman's cloak and she walked away a bit. The foxy woman stooped for a stone and struck her. When the woman went home, she saw a bit of a basin on to her cloak and it was with that the foxy woman struck her. Máire went away for the cure. She arrived soon afterwards with it. She cured the woman that time. But she could not get up on the wedding day.

Collector: Pádruig Ó Síothcháin, Caherkeen, Co. Cork

Long ago there was a man in Eyeries named Partlan. He used be always vexing Máire Ní Mhurchadha. He had a public house in the village. One day Máire was inside in his house, and he began vexing her. He said to her that she used to go with the fairies so that she would get a glass of whiskey and a good dinner. She did not say anything but walked out the door. When she was going, she said to him, "I'll let you," and away she went. A few days afterwards he got a cask of whisky. That night when he went to bed. He heard a great noise downstairs as if the cask was leaking away. He jumped out of the bed and went down. He went into the kitchen he did not see any person. Then he went into the shop and no sooner was he inside then he was taken with a kick. A crowd caught him and dragged him out of the shop and into the kitchen. They tried to put him into the fireplace. Others tried to drag him out the back door, and others tried to bring him out the front door. They kept him there till he was worn out, and at last they left him go. He went to bed again and told all his adventures to his wife. He had all the blame on Maire Ní Mhurchadha. He said he would get up with the dawn in the morning and go out before Maire would come. When morning came, he got up and dressed himself. He did not make any fire for fear Maire would see the smoke. Then he opened the door to go out and there was Maire sitting near the door. "Well," says she, "How are you after the night?" The man did not say anything.

Collector: Áine Ní Dhuibhir, Urhin, Co. Cork
Informant: Maire Bean Uí Aractain, grandmother, Ardacluggin, Co. Cork

Gortfhathaigh Cathairchuim Árd a' Chloiginn

It is supposed that long ago two giants had a fight in Gortfhathaigh and the fight lasted for four hours. One of them was stronger than the other. The weaker one jumped from his opponent to Rahish and the print of his foot is to be seen on a rock there always. The strong one followed him, then the weaker one jumped from there to Carrigíll and the other one caught him there and threw his head off and it came down on Árd' a Chloiginn and his body came into Tráigh 'n Bháid. It was buried in Jim Harrington's field and three golláin stood to mark the grave, two to his feet and one to his head.

Collector: Diarmuid Ó Dubhgáin, Caherkeen, Co. Cork
Informant: Séamus Ó Dubhgáin, father

Stolen by Fairies

Not very long ago there lived a man and his wife in Ardgroom. The man's name was Jim Durd. Once his wife was taken away by the fairies. The man did not know that she was taken away because there was another woman put in her place. The woman that was put in her place was sick in the bed. The two women were alike in every way, so he thought that it was his wife was there. Máire Ní Mhurchadha told the man to go over to Kerry and that he would get his wife there. She told him that there would be a horse race there and to watch the second last horse. She said that his wife would be behind a man on the horse. She said when the horse would come to grab his wife off the horse or otherwise he would not get her. He got a boat and a crew of men and went over to Kerry. He did what Máire Ní Mhurchadha told him to do. When the horse came along, he grabbed his wife off the horse. He brought her to the boat and went away home with her. When he went home the other woman was gone before him. His wife lived for a few years after that.

A Strange Light in Eyeries

Once there was a priest in Eyeries Parish. One night this priest was to Inchinteskin on a sick call. When he was going home the man of the house conveyed him as far as the priest's house. When they came down to the main road, they met five young children. The man said to the priest, "Isn't it late these children are out?" "Mind your own business," said the priest. They walked away and when they were a little farther a light shone on their faces. The priest got afraid. He walked away and he brought the man away with him. When they were to the west of Mike Cronin's house a light shone in a field below the road. There is a rock standing in that field still. It is said it was on that night the rock was put there. The priest went home, and he brought the man with him and kept him for the night. The priest died shortly afterwards.

A Mysterious Horse

Long ago there lived in Kilmacowen a boy and his mother. They had land and cattle south in Béal Na Leabchan. Every morning, before day, the boy used to go to see the cattle. One morning when he was going he met a horse. The horse would not let the boy pass. The boy tried every way to pass but he could not. At last, he went on the horse and the horse carried him to Béal na Leabchan to see the cattle and back. The horse let the boy off in the same spot where he took him on. The boy went home, and it was not long afterwards till he died.

Collector: Seán Ó Néill, Coulagh, Co. Cork

The Ghostly Priest

Long ago there was a parish clerk in Eyeries. This clerk's home was in Kilcatherine. He went home every night and came back in the morning to do his work. One morning he came at dawn. As the people of the village were not up, he decided on going into the church. When he was inside a little while, he went to sleep. Having slept a while, he heard a voice saying, "Is there anyone here who would answer Mass." This voice was heard three times. The clerk got up, went up to the altar, and answered Mass. When Mass was finished the priest spoke and said that he was going to be in the church for ever until he would get someone to answer Mass for him. When he was in this life, he got money to say a Mass and he neglected it.

Collector: Siobhan Ní Murachada, Caherkeen, Co. Cork
Informant: Sean Ó Murachadha, father, aged 50

The Dancing Spirit

Once there was a boy coming home from his work when he met a spirit. The spirit began to dance in front of him. The boy caught her, brought her home and put her sitting near the fire. He said that she should be his wife's bridesmaid. The spirit was trying to go away and said she would give him a crock of gold if he would leave her go, and that nothing would happen him coming back. He said he would leave her go. She brought him to a field, took up a stone and under it was a crock of gold which she used to take from the people coming from town and kill them. The boy went home and got married and he was rich all his life.

Collector: Siobhan Ní Murachadha, Caherkeen, Co. Cork
Informant: Sean Ó Murchadha, father, aged 50

Droichead na Gadaidhe

About ninety years ago, when the famine was in the country and the food was very scarce, the people were in the habit of stealing cattle. There was a man that used always steal cattle and sometime after his death he was seen standing in a river near the bridge called Droichead na Ghadaidhe. It happened that another man who used also steal cattle was passing along and he saw the man standing in the river with a stick in his hand. He asked the man why was he standing in the river with a stick in his hand. The other man told him that he was suffering his purgatory and that he should stay there till green buds would come on his stick. Then the other man asked him what did he do, and he told him that he used steal cattle. Then the other man jumped into the river and said he would also stay till his stick would sprout. That is the reason why the bridge is called Droichead na Ghadaidhe

Stealing the Butter

Long ago, a woman went to a neighbour's house for a jug of milk. She got it and she brought it home and threw it into her own small cream tub. It happened that the woman whom she took the milk from was making a churn on that day and they were all trying to make it, but no butter came on it, and at last they had to leave it. The old woman said that she knew who took the butter away that it was the woman who took the jug of milk. The next morning, she went to the woman's house for the milk, but she was not at home. She waited till she came back. When she came the other woman told her to give her as much milk as she took from her the previous morning, and she did. When she reached home, she threw it into her own churn and after a quarter of an hour the churn was made.

Collector: Aine Ní Duibhir, Urhin
Informant: Maire Bean Ní Aractain, aged 74, grandmother, Ardacluggin

A rock in Gort Athaigh

Long ago there was a rock in Gort Athaigh. That rock was thrown across from Kerry to that place behind the hill. It was about eight-ton weight. Once a man was building a house. He had a crowd of men working. He said to them, "Wouldn't that be a fine stone for the corner of the house." Then the men got crowbars and went to take up the stone. They put the crowbars under it and raised it up. They saw a lot of rosary beads under it. One of them men said to leave it there that they would get some other stone for the corner of the house. A part of that rock is still to be seen.

Collector: Cait Ní Suileabain, Caherkeen, Co. Cork
Informant: Cait Bean Ní Suilleabháin, mother, aged 40

The Lost Daughter

Long ago there lived in Glenbeag a man named Crowley. The people boycotted him for some reason or other. He used come to Mass every Sunday and after Mass he used stay behind the church until everybody used to go home. An old man came to him one Sunday and said, "There you are Mr Crowley. I know you are a good brave man and if you will do what I tell you, the people will come to like you. There is a Líos in Bofficle and if you will come there tonight and go in the opening, they will be dancing and singing there and enjoy yourself with them. They will offer you food but don't take any from them. They will ask you to cross to Kerry with them playing a hurley match. Choose a hurley for yourself and go with them."

About twelve o'clock they left the Líos and went down to Ballycrovane. They launched a boat there and went across to Kerry. They were met by the Kerry team. They marched together to the field and played the match, and Crowley played a great match and won the game for them. They went back to Ballycrovane and Crowley went home.

He went to Mass the next Sunday and after mass the old man came to him again and said, "You did a brave act last Sunday night, and now there is another task before you tonight. There are six men going over to Kerry for a girl. She is a lonely daughter, her father has none but her. They will come by road with her and if you are brave enough you will take her off them. If you would stay in a lonely part of the road, that is east of the boundary, they will be coming about one o'clock in the night. You will hear them coming as they will be coming quickly. They will have the coffin on their shoulders. Have a stick in your hand, pull the coffin from their shoulders and threaten them to keep clear of you or you'll strike them with the stick. Don't be afraid of them. Take off the lid of the coffin and take out the girl and take her home with you. There will be an old woman in her place until you get back with the girl."

He did as the old man told him and a few days after he went home with the girl. As they were nearing the house Crowley said he would go in first and break the news. So, he went in and asked the man how his daughter was getting on. The old man said she was very bad. He asked could himself be left to see her. He went to the bed and there was the old person lying very sick in bed. He said to the man, "This is not your daughter is here." Then he said to the old person "Get out of the bed," but she only groaned. He said again, "get out of the bed or I will put the poker in the fire." He left the room to put the poker in the fire and when he came back, she was gone. So, Crowley got married to the girl and lived happy for the rest of his life.

Collector: Máire Ní Arachtáin, Caherkeen, Co. Cork
Informant: Micheál Ó Arachtáin, aged 50, farmer

A Ghostly Boat

One night long ago seiners were going fishing. The sea was very rough, and they were afraid to go out. When they were a long way out and the boats were full of fish, a great storm arose and they had to dump the fish again. The boats were struck against the rocks, and it was so dark that the seiners did not know where they were. Then they saw a great big light coming towards them. When it came nearer it seemed like a boat with a great light on one side of it. They saw men dressed in white and they pulling the oars very fast. The boat was a long way out from them, and it kept before them until they came to Tráigh an Bháid. The seiners were frightened. They watched to see where would the boat go. It went away out and then it disappeared. They said that it was some boat came to show them the way and only for the boat coming they would be drowned.

The Milk Stealing Hare

There was a man there long ago and he had eight cows but he could not make any butter. A woman came up to him one day and she told him to go next morning to the field and that he would see a hare milking the cows. She told him get the two best hounds in the village and to kill the hare. The next morning the man went to the field, and he saw the hare milking the cows. He killed the hare with the two hounds. The woman told him that herself would not be at home when he would come back and if he would kill the hare to bring him home and boil him. When the hare was about boiled the man looked into the pot to see if it was boiled. There was nothing in the pot but water and he heard the screaming up the chimney all that day and the woman was the hare herself and she was killed long ago by dogs.

Collector: Síobhán Ní Arachtáin, Caherkeen, Co. Cork
Informant: Mícheál Ó Arachtáin, father, aged 50, farmer

The Sick Wife

Long ago there was a woman, and she was not feeling well in the mind. Her husband told her to go to Loch a Cuinleán to see would she get better. So, she went, and she remained there that night. When she was coming home the next day it was dark. When she was coming along, she met a man riding on a horse. He asked her would she come up behind him on the horse and she said she would, that she was tired. After a long journey, as they were going towards her house, the boy asked her did she know him. She said she did not. He then told her that he was her son that died years ago. He also told her that a cow died that morning belong to her in the field of the líos and that they brought her home and boiled a piece of her to eat. "When you go home," he said, "tell them to throw her away, that she was not your cow was there, but another old animal put there instead of her.

Collector: Síobhán Ní Arachtáin, Caherkeen, Co. Cork
Informant: Eibhléan Bean ui Arachtáin, mother, aged 38

The Stolen Horse

Once there was a man in Cahirkeem. He went to his uncle's house one day. It was twelve o'clock when he left his uncle's house. His uncle was trying to keep him for the night, but he would not stay. On his way home the horse began screaming and running away with him. He was trying to keep the horse back, but he could not. When he was coming near the house, he knew that the horse saw something before him on the road. Then himself saw something out in the middle of the road and it looked like an animal. The horse passed out and the animal sat down on the road. When the man looked back, he could not see the animal. When he went home his horse fell dead. Then he knew that the animal he saw on the road was like his own horse. So, it was how his horse was taken away by the fairies.

Collector: Síobhán Ní Arachtáin, Caherkeen, Co. Cork
Informant: Séamus Ó Arachtáin, aged 50

A Crowd in the Night

One day my grandmother went to town across the hill with a pan of butter. It was late in the night when she was coming across the hill. When she was coming down the hill, she heard great noise but she did not see anyone. When she was nearly home a crowd of people passed her and they were running, they had a football. One of them said to her not to be out so late any other night or she would be killed. She got very weak, and when she came home, she could not open the door. She went around the house and she started calling somebody to open the door for her. She heard the door opening and she came around the house and she went in, and when she came inside the door, she began telling them what she saw on the hill. She got a weakness and she died. The crowd of people was telling her that she would die and that there would be a crowd in her wake.

Collector: Máire Ní Shúilleabháin, Inchinteskin, Co. Cork
Informant: Padrúig ó Shuilleabháin, father, aged 52, farmer

Unwelcome Guests

Long ago there was a house in Cahirkeem and the fairies use to be coming in every night after they going to bed. The fairies used to be dancing, playing and noising the cups. One night they were breaking the cups and the man of the house came down from the bed and he asked them what were they doing and that himself could not sleep with the noise they had going on. One of the fairies said that they would not leave the house until they had five years spent in the house, and after five years they left the house. The man of the house could not make any butter while they were in the house. When they left the house, he could make the butter from that on. When the fairies went to the other house, they never left it and the people of the house had to leave it and go to some other house. The fairies were there in the house for a long time but there is no sight of them there now.

The Fairy Girl

Long ago there lived a woman and her son together and there was an old, ruined castle not far from their house. The people used to say that the castle used be lit up every November's night by the fairies. This boy told his mother that he would go to the castle on the next November's night. His mother told him not to go. But he went. When he was going near it, he saw the castle all lights. He went as far as the window, and he looked in. One of the fairies called him by his own name. He went in and he was playing with the fairies. About one o'clock in the night the fairies asked him would he come to Dublin for a girl. He said how could he go, and they said that he would go with them.

When they went to Dublin one of the fairies threw a piece of timber in the window and the girl came out. They brought the girl away home with them. When they were coming near the castle the boy asked the fairies would himself bring the girl for them and they gave him the girl. When they were going near the boy's house, he would not give them the girl. They were trying to take the girl from him, but they could not. One of the fairies said that the girl would not be of any use to him. He went away home running and the fairies after him, but they could not take the girl from him.

When he went home, his mother asked him where did he get the girl but he would not tell her. She could not speak or do anything and after months she began working but she could not speak. The next November's night he went to the castle again. One of the fairies was standing in the door and she said to him that the girl would be of no use to him until she get three drops of the bottle she had in her hand. He snapped the bottle she had in her hand and ran home with it. When he went home, he gave three drops of the bottle to the girl and then she could talk and do everything from that on. The next day the girl said that she would go back to her own house in Dublin herself with the boy.

When they went to the girls home her father came out and the girl asked him did he know her, but her father said he did not know her. She said that she was his daughter, and he said that his daughter was dead and buried with a year. Then the girl told her father to call out her mother and when her mother came out the girl asked her did she know her, but her mother said she did not. Then the girl said did she know the ring was on her finger and her mother said that was her daughter's ring. So, they left the girl and boy into the house and they told what happened to her. They lived very happy from that on.

Collector: Siobhán Ní Arachtáin, Caherkeen, Co. Cork
Informant: Michéal Ó Arachtáin, father, aged 50

The Missing Tobacco

Long ago there was a man in Cahirkeem and he was making a rick of hay. He had a crowd of men making the rick with him. After dinner the man left his tobacco on the window and himself and all the men went out at the hay. A spell after they going out the woman saw the tobacco all eaten so she said to herself, "If I caught the one that ate it he would get it from me," and she heard the voice saying, "There is no tobacco for that man because I wanted it." So, she put the tobacco in the window again and it was taken. When the man came in, he asked for the tobacco and the woman told him what she heard the voice saying, and he said that it was a fairy that wanted it and he heard a voice saying, I am your brother, and he told him to pray for him. The man of the house used to say a prayer for him every night. So, he was never since heard of or seen.

A Ghost Story

Long ago there was a man from Cahirkeem working in Allihies mines. He was going home one Saturday night. He was very anxious for a smoke, but he had no match to light his pipe. Then he saw a fire on the road before him. While he was lighting his pipe, he saw a man coming to him. They walked on together until they came to Eyeries but they never spoke. He went into a public house for a drink. The ghost waited outside. He offered a drink to the ghost, but he did not take it. They walked on again till they came to Ballycrovane. Then the ghost spoke. "Well," he said, "We must separate now from each other. I must be in Waterford before the cockcrow, and you will be going home to Cahirkeem. I will give you advice not to be out late any Saturday night from this out. Be off with you now," said the ghost, "for a crowd of people will be going this way soon and if they catch you out you will pay for it." The ghost shook hands with him. Then he looked into the ghost he knew him He was a neighbour from the village who died six years ago. He went off and did not see him since. The man was gone a quarter of a mile when he heard the great noise after him. He did nothing but throw himself into a thicket of brambles. He was not long there when away down came the great noise. There were horses. There they were knocking sparks out of the road. There were gentleman and ladies there. He knew some of them. They all went away, and the man got out of his hiding and away home with him. Just when he reached home it was cock crow and his wife asked him did anything happen to him, she said the cock was crowing all night. He did not tell the story to her until a few days after.

Collector: Cáit Ní Shuilebháin, Caherkeen, Co. Cork
Informant: Cáit Bean Ní Shuileabháin

The Pedlars

There were two pedlars in Urhan long ago. One day they were going to a fair and they saw a dead man on one side of the road, and he had a fine pair of boots on him. They were trying to take off the boots and they could not. So, one of them cut the two legs off the man and put them into a bag and they went away. They separated from each other that night. They went to two farmers houses. The pedlar that had the boots in the bag went to a house where there were five cows tied on one side of it. When the farmer went to bed that night. The pedlar made a fine fire and put on it a big pot of water, and put the two legs of the man into the pot and when they softened, he took off the boots and he threw the legs of the man under one of the cow's heads. Then he went away before the farmer got up. When the farmer got up in the morning, he did not see any pedlar and he saw the two legs of the man under the cow's head, and he thought it was the cow eaten the pedlar. After a while the other pedlar came in looking for the other one. He asked the farmer where did he go, and he said he was not there at all when he got up. The peddler saw the two legs of the man under the cow's head, and he said to the farmer you must have killed him, and he said he would go and tell the police. The farmer said he would give him money and the pedlar said will you give me much. The farmer said he would give him twenty pounds if he would not tell the police. The farmer gave him the money and the pedlar went away. When he was going on the road the other pedlar jumped out from inside the fence and the two went away. They went into a public house, and they rose a spree. The shopkeeper asked them where did they get the money and one of the pedlars told her about the farmer. The shopkeeper told the police, and the police sent for the farmer and the two pedlars got jail.

Collector: Cáit Ní Domhnuidhe, Urhin, Co. Cork
Informant: Micheal Ó Domhnuidhe

A Knock at the Door

One night long ago there was a big crowd of people in a house sitting around the fire telling stories. After a while the woman of the house heard a knock at the door, and she told the rest that somebody was knocking but they heard nothing. After a while the crowd went away, and the man of the house came in and his wife asked him if he heard or saw anything, and he said he did not. Then she told him that she heard the knock at the door. He said he would go out to the stable to see the horse. When he was opening the door of the stable, a horse got up of the fence and walked down the garden. When he went into the stable his own horse was dead. He said it was how his own horse was swept.

Collector: Máire Ní Shúilleabháin

URHAN
People, Places and Property

Morty Óg

Morty Óg lived in Eyeries Beag. It was Morty Óg that shot Puxley near the gates of Dunboy. He was fighting in the battle of Culloden. He was not married at all. But there was a man living in the house with him. His surname was Harrington. When he shot Puxley there was a man with him. Puxley was on horseback when Morty shot him. Out through an old window of an old cabhlac he shot him. Puxley was passing on the horse. The soldiers heard that Morty shot Puxley and they came the next day across the hill and down to his house. Harrington was in the house when the soldiers surrounded them. He ran out the back door and down across a field. He jumped across the river and the next moment his head was blown off. The soldiers thought that he was Morty Óg.

They caught Morty above in his own house. Then the soldiers brought him down to Feora. There was an old horse feeding on the banks of the river and they threw him across the horse, and the horse brought him to Castletownbere to the pier. They tied Morty on to a ship and dragged him to Cork. Then they cut off his head and spiked it on the gates of the Cork jail. He had a son whose name was Morty na n-Ínse. He was going to Cork once and near Kenmare he asked for lodgings, and he got them. When he got up the next morning three robbers came to the door. He had a revolver with him, and they had nothing. He told them put up their hands or that he would shoot them. Then he tied their hands and he marched them up to Cork ahead of him and gave them to the soldiers. The soldiers told him that they would give him anything he asked. He asked them to take down his father's head off the spike and they did. When the soldiers shot Harrington, it was not long before it when the priest cursed him. One Sunday the two of them were coming from town and when they were coming, Mass was going on in a little Church near the bridge, near John Lynch's meadow, and they sat on the fence outside laughing at the people.

There was an old man outside the door praying and Harrington put dirt into his gun and fired at the old man and burnt all his hair. The people were laughing and after Mass the priest asked the people why they were laughing, and someone told. Then the priest cursed in Irish. He said "Ran na Raithnighe ortha siúd." When Morty shot Puxley the wife was with him, and Harrington said, "leagfá gé nuair leagais an gandal." Morty said he would never shoot a woman.

Collector: Seán Ó Súilleabháin, Coulagh, Co. Cork
Informant: Mícheál Ó Súilleabháin, Grandparent

James Sullivan

There was a man in Cahirkeem named James Sullivan. He was a great swimmer. One day there was a heavy gale, and the wind was taking his house and he had a ladder trying to fix the house. The wind took the ladder and brought it into the sea. He swam out for it about a mile and brought it back with him.

A Great Step-Dancer

There was a man named Jim Shea living in Cahirkeem. He was a great step dancer. He used be dancing in the weddings and other dances. He used be out fishing all the time himself with other men. They used live in the boat. They had their own food in the boat. There were bunks in the boat. One day they were coming over from Kerry and they met with an accident and Tim fell out of the boat and got drowned. His wife and children were great dancers and singers also. One morning the mother was found dead in the bed. All the children went away to America and my father bought their farm.

Collector: Siobhán Ní Mhúrcadha, Caherkeen, Co. Cork
Informant, Maighread Ní Mhúrcadha, mother

Tobar Beanniughthe

There is a well in Eyeries. It is called Tobairín Beanniughthe. It is connected with St Finian. Long ago people used to pay rounds there on May Day or on holidays if there would be anything wrong with them such as sore eyes or sore throat. When they would have a sore eye, they would make the sign of the cross over it with the water of the well. If they would have a sore throat, they would drink the holy water. When the rich people would go to it, they would leave money there, and when the young people would go to it, they would leave a piece of cotton there. Some of the people used to bring home little bottles of it. There is no water in it now.

Collector: Pádruig Ó Síothcháin, Kilcatherine, Co. Cork
Informant: Máire Ní Shíothcháin, grandmother, Caherkeen, Co. Cork

Kilmacowen

In the townland of Castletownbere there is a place called Kilmacowen and this is how it got its name. In olden days it is supposed that a wealthy king named Owen had a strong fortress built in the outskirts of this village. He had a son called Mac Owen. This boy sailed for Spain where he met the beautiful daughter of the Spanish king. She was called the Princess Béara and she eloped with Mac Owen from her father's house. They sailed for Ireland and landed in Rosmacowen. They married and went to live in Mac Owen's Castle. When the Spanish King heard he was furious. He and his troops sailed for Ireland and landed in Kenmare Bay. They came from the north and Mac Owen and his wife fled, but they were killed. The Spaniards destroyed the castle, buried Mac Owen near it and then departed bringing with them the body of the Princess Béara. Chill means burying place, therefore Kilmacowen means the burying place of Mac Owen.

Collector: Miceal Ó Mhurchadha, Kilcatherine, Co. Cork
Informant: Séan Ó Mhurchadha

URHAN
Farming, Trade and Crafts

Spinning and Weaving

First they shear the sheep and wash the wool, and leave it out a few days until it gets white. When it is white, they get two things with teeth on it and put the wool in between them called carders and be rubbing it until they make it in rolls. When it is all in one stitch they roll it in one ball and get a spinning wheel and put two stitches together and spin it. When it is spun, they make stockings and jumpers and wash them again because they are all oily. Some people wash it after spinning it. There is a woman yet in Cahirkeem and she is carding and spinning it herself, her name is Mrs Harrington.

Flax

Everyone used to sow flax long ago. When the flax used be ripe they used to pull it from the root. They used to put it over in Locha Lín to steep. It used to be left there for two weeks. Then they used to put it bleaching in a bare field for three or four days. Then they used to strike it down on a stone with a túairgín to soften it. A túairgín was a piece of oak. Then they used to pull it through a hackle (taisteal) to clean it. A hackle is an iron thing with long spikes. Darby Gabha used to make hackles. He had a forge in Coulagh. Then they used to settle it on the wall for the weaver and he used to do the rest of it. The people used to make sheets of it.

Collector: Pádruig Ó Cróinín, Kilcatherine, Co. Cork
Informant: Micheál Ó Cróinín, Coulagh, Co. Cork

Seaweed

Carraigín moss: People pick it in the summer. They spread it in a field until it gets white. Then they boil it and eat it.

Míobhán: People pick it and let it dry and eat it.

Duilisc: Kind of míobhán. It grows in long narrow leaves. It is not very nice to eat.

Triopán: People pick it and boil it and then eat it. It grows about the size of míobhán. The colour of it is kind of brown.

Feamnach: It is cut or pulled off the rocks and left in a heap for about a week or a fortnight. Then it is put on the ridges after setting the sgiolláns.

Collector: Seán Ó Néill, Coulagh, Co. Cork

Making Butter

Long ago the people used to make butter. The butter they used to have left after themselves they used put it into barrels called firkins. When the firkin would be full of butter, they used to bring it to town. The days they used to go was called the firkin day. When they would come from town the firkin used be scrubbed with heather. They used put a pot of water on the fire and put salt on the cover of the pot. After washing it they would not use the pot for anything else. They used wash the churn with the water and put the heather under the cream tub as it was custom.

Home Industries

Long ago the women used to be spinning every night. The men used to be making súgán stools which they called suidhestíns from the hay. They used to make their own nets for fishing and their own candles. There are only a few spinning wheels around now. Long ago there used to be one in every house. First, they used to get the wool and card it. Some people used to bring in the weaver and they used to spin it and make it into thread. They used to keep some of the thread for stockings, and dye more of it. They used to knit trousers. When they used to have it spun, they used to make chains of it and the men and boys used to make balls of it. There was a mill in Eyeries. Then they used put it to the mill to be woven into cloth. Then they used put it to the tucker and it used to be made into frieze. The men used to make the súgans for the cocks of hay and for the suidhestíns. First, they used get hay and get a big rod and bend it and put a rope across it and then put a handle in it and keep twisting it and keep adding the hay on to the cruaicín according to want. They used call the rod a cruaicín.

They used to make baskets which they used to call caiseáns. Everyone used to have the trees for making baskets. They used to call them twigs. First, they used to make a bundle of them and put a súgán around them. Then put it into a hole of water for nine or ten days. The reason why they put them into water is that when they will make the caiseán that the rods will bend without breaking. Then they make the baskets. They still make baskets. First, they used to cut eighteen sticks the same size and put them standing in a row. Then they used to make the bottom of it, and they used to leave a hole in the bottom for every stick. Then the used to get a thin stick and tied it on to every row. Then they kept adding on the rods until they came to the middle. Then they left a space on the middle. They put a rod slant ways on the space. Then they start to do the same thing from the space to the top of it.

Collector: Siobhán Ní Mhurchadha

URHAN
Leisure

Games

They used play pickey long ago. They used put a line of stones after one another and hop around them. They used play thaws and buttons. The way they used play thaws, they used stand a reel on the floor and leave go the thaw at the reel and if they would knock it, it would be game. The way they used play button, they used get a button and go around to everyone with the button and leave the button fall into someone's hand and then ask what hand was the button in and the one that would be wrong would get a slap, and the one that would be right would go around with the button again. They used play another game. They used get a stick and burn it in the fire and when it would be red take it out and spit on it, and the one that would quench it, the rest would say cuirfidh an trom trom ort, and they would put the chairs and stools on the top of his back. They used play Mooten Buidhe. They used stand a stick in the middle of the field and they used get a stick and try to knock it and the one that would knock it would back away and the rest would try to catch him.

Collector: Máire Ní Shuilibháin, Inchinteskin, Co. Cork
Informant: Maighread Ní Shuilibháin, mother, Inchinteskin, Co. Cork

URHAN
Local Customs

Rushes

Long ago the people used to make candles themselves. First, they used melt lard or tallow. When it was melted, they poured it into the dipping pan. These pans were called moulds (sligire) Then they got rushes and peeled them and left a strip of the green in to keep it firm. Then they dipped one of the rushes into the dipping pan. Then they let it stand there until it got hard. They made them about fourteen inches long. They did not last long because they were very soft. They used them as lanterns going to see the cattle, and when going to many other places.

Collector: Pádruig Ó Síothcháin, Kilcatherine, Co. Cork
Informant: Máire Ní Shíothcháin, Grandparen't, Caherkeen, Co. Cork

Customs of May Day

There are many pishogues about May Day. In the morning before the sun rises green branches are brought into the house to show the beginning of summer. They put out a white handkerchief before day and bring it in afterwards and if anybody is sick, rub it to them and it will cure them. If a cow should calf on May Day, they say that the cow and the calf would die. It was also a practice not to put outside the door any red fire or ashes. They say everyone should make a churn on May Eve and not on May Day.

Collector: Seosaimh Ó Mhurchadha, Caherkeen, Co. Cork

Old Customs

Long ago the old people on St Patrick's Day morning used to put a cross on the cows' foreheads. They'd burn a saileach in the fire and when it would get black, they used to make the sign of the cross on their shoulders. They used turn up the bottom of the churn and make the sign of the cross with tar on it. On Mayday morning whoever would be first to the well before the sun gets up should bring in a bucket of water and should put one basin of it in the milk-house. They should wash the pans with the rest of it for luck. On Mayday morning in olden times the old people used to lock the door of the cowhouse for fear the cows would be milked. They used lock the door of the milk-house for fear the milk or the butter would be removed. They used to bring in green branches. When the first cow used calf, they used put the first milk over the fire and make the sign of the cross with the right hand over it.

Collector: Peadar Ó hÚrdail, Kilcatherine, Co. Cork

Churning

It is said that it is not right to let a spark of fire out of the house while a churn is being made. If a person should enter a house while a churn is being made, and if he should not strike any blow in the churn, and if he should walk out, it is said that the butter would not come in the churn.

There was a churn being made in a house long ago. A neighbour came in to redden his pipe. He walked out soon after and he did not strike any blow in the churn. The butter was coming in the churn. The people of the house were trying to make the churn, but it was no use for them. That churn did not make or a good many other churns after that. The man of the house was told to go to the house of the neighbour that came in to redden his pipe. He went out one morning and the excuse he gave was that his fire was out. He got a spark of fire and his churns made for him after that.

Collector: Seán Ó Néill, Coulagh, Co. Cork
Informant: Bríghid Ní Néill, Grandparent

How the people used to make the tea long ago

Out of Caisreabhán the people used to make the tea long ago. It was only the sick people that used to drink it. It was a very bitter drink. They used to gather it in Feora. It used to be in big, long strips. They used to pull it with their hands and gather it with their aprons. It was mostly women that used gather it. They used to make heaps of it over in the old point and when they would have enough gathered, they would spread it out in the gravel where the tide used not go over to rot it, and to dry it the people used to spread it. They used to leave it there for two or three days and it used to turn brown. Then they used to bring it back and put it into brown paper bags and put it over the fire. When they used want a drink of it always they used put their hand up and take down a big fist of it, then they used get a pot of boiling water and throw the fist of tea into it. They used leave it drawing for a half an hour. When it used be drawn they used get a timber jug and fill it with tea, then they used throw a drop of milk in it but no sugar. A pot of it used to do them for a week.

Flummery

Flummery was used in most houses some years ago. It was a healthy and delicious drink either by drinking it warm or leaving it till next day to jelly, it was delicious with cream. It was made by steeping two cups of oatmeal in cold water for a couple of hours, then pouring into a bowl of jelly and adding sugar and cream to taste while boiling.

Collector: Anstí Ní Shúilleabháin

Stampy and Starch

Long ago the people used to make stampy cakes from potatoes. Out of the black potatoes they used to make stampy. They used to get a scraper and scrape all the dirt and skin off them. They used to make starch also out of potatoes. They used to boil them. When they used to be boiled, they used to get a flannel rag and bruise them in the rag. They used to get a clean bucket and put it under the potatoes when they used to be bruising them. Then water used to drop out of them and into the bucket for a night and it used to thicken up. Then they used to get a saucepan and throw a fist of it into the saucepan and boil it. When it used be boiled they used take it up and leave it get cold, and it used to turn into powder. Then they used to mix it with blue and throw it into boiling water. Then they used to rub it to the shirts, and it used to make them very hard. The cakes they used to make out of the stampy used to be very tough. There used to be a gridle or two in every house. When the cakes used to be baked, they used to cut them up in quarters, and they used to get a fork and a knife to tear it out of each other.

Collector: Seán Ó Súilleabháin, Coulagh, Co. Cork

Saint Martin's Eve

Saint Martin's Eve falls on the 10th of November. Long ago on that night in the year 1700 the people used to go out setting their nets. One night while they were setting their nets, they saw a man rise up out of the water and he riding on a horse. He went towards them and while he was going towards them, he waved his hand towards the land. The men of one of the boats said that they would cut their nets and they did. So, they pulled away to the land. When they reached the land, a storm arose. The crew of the other boat were lost. Some of the old men used not go out on that night ever since, and the young people would stay inside on that night, and the old people used to tell them to stay inside that something would happen to them. And it is supposed that it was Saint Martin that was there.

Collector: Diarmuid Ó Dubhgáin, Kilcatherine, Co. Cork
Informant: Séamus Ó Dubhgáin, father, Caherkeen, Co. Cork

May Day

There are lots of pishogues about May Day. In the morning before the sun rises, green branches are brought into the house to show the beginning of the summer. If you put out a white handkerchief before day and bring it in afterwards and if anybody is sick to rub it to them it will cure them. If a cow will calf on May Day, they say the cow and calf will die. On May Day some people light a blessed candle under the cows to bless them. If you spill a drop of milk on May Day, they say you will be spilling it for the year. They say you should not give away any milk on May Day or May Eve because you would not have luck, but if you make it on May Eve you will have luck on your butter. If you put a churn outside the door on May Day and turn it to the neighbour's door you will take away their butter. It is also a practice not to put outside the door any red ashes or a man to put out his pipe lighting. Nobody ever gets married on May Day.

Fishing customs

Long ago, when the people used to go seining, the people of the house used throw an old shoe after them for luck. They used to make the sign of the cross with holy water before leaving the house. When the men used pick the stones for to stop the fish they used not pick any white stone. Fishermen do not start the season on a Monday night. If a seine should have a big haul of fish on Sunday night, it would be a bad sign for the rest of the week.

Collector: Micheal Ó Mhurcadha
Informant: Séan Mhurcadha

The Food the People Used to Have Long Ago

When the men used rise in the morning, they used to go out working. When the women used get up, they used to bake a cake and boil gruel. The cakes were made of flour mixed with meal or sometimes stampy. The men used to come in about nine or ten o'clock and have their breakfast. Then they used to go out working again. They used come in about three o'clock and have their dinner. They used to have potatoes and fish or sometimes meat for their dinner. They used always kill a pig or a cow for the winter. They used not have any supper. They used do with their dinner at about three o'clock until their breakfast at about ten o'clock in the morning. Sometimes they used to have gruel at nightfall. They used not have any tea. In winter they used to have uisge te salainn. That was hot water mixed with milk and salt. When they used to be cutting turf in a bog, they used to have cans of curds and sweet milk. Sometimes they used to have coffee in the morning.

Collector: Seán Ó Néill, Coulagh, Co. Cork

URHAN
Sea and Shipwrecks

Drownings

There were five men drowned in Cahirkeen about 78 years ago. One night there was a seine out fishing. They were coming over by Gortfhathaig and near Daingean, and the follower was over-flowing with fish. The sea was a little rough and two waves came in at each side of the follower and sank it. There were six men in the follower and five were drowned and one man came safe. He took off his coat and tied it to the boat and kept a hold on it. They would all be saved only that the seine boat went away from them. One man kept struggling away in the water. His name was Jack McAuliffe. The five men were seen on the rock until the one man got saved. There was another seine-boat in the strand and they heard the calling and they resuced him. As soon as they took him in the boat, the follower was made in pieces against a rock.

Two men got drowned in Cahirkeem. Their names were Pat Fenton and Dan Sullivan. They both went to Lauragh by sea for a boat-load of timber. They left Lauragh about eight o clock. It was in the wintertime. Their boat was too heavy, the sea got wild, and the boat got capsized outside Ardgroom. On their way home and the men were lost. On the following morning the boat was found floating in the water. Then the news came that they were drowned, and it went around the place. Fenton was a boat builder and he was a native of Kerry. He lived in Cahirkeem with his wife and family. His wife died shortly after, and the family had to leave as they had no land. Dan Sullivan was in America for about ten years, and after coming home he lived with his father and mother. It was very sad, their bodies were never found and their friends felt very sad. It happened about eleven years ago.

Collector: Seosamh Ó Murchú, Caherkeen, Co. Cork
Informant: Seán Ó Murchadha, father

Long ago a man lived in Cahirkeem named Paddy Goggin. One day himself and five other men went across to Kerry with a boat of salted fish. When they were as far as a rock called Billig Mór na Bhera, the boat struck the rock and the boat turned. They were all lost. That day Mrs Goggin was over to Mrs Downing's shop, and Fr O'Reilly came in. He said, "How are you Mrs. Goggin?" She said, "How would I be when my husband is by the sharks of the sea?" She then said to try to find him, dead or alive, in God's honour. He had to do something, and he asked her, "Did he bless himself after the last meal?" and if he did, he could be found. The next day the priest got a crew of men and went out. He asked the men to show him where the drowning took place. When they went to the place the priest took out something. When he left it in the water it went round in a circle and then sank. A few days after a man from Gort was down to the strand for weeds and the body came in with the weeds.

In the year of 1924 two men went to Kerry for timber, they were living in Cahirkeem. When they were coming home the night got very dark and the sea got rough, and they got drowned. About a week before they got drowned one of them was seen in some place that he was never there before, and the person that saw him asked him was he in such a place, and he was not, that he was in one of the neighbour's houses that night, and the person that saw him said that he was there. Next day after the two men being drowned, the people saw the boat floating outside on the sea, and they went out for it. When they saw the boat, they it knew it was the boat the two men had going to Kerry, and they knew the two men were lost and were never got since. They never came into any strand like the other men that used to be drowned.

Collector: Siobán Ní Aractáin, Caherkeen, Co. Cork
Informant: Micéal Ó Aractháin, father, aged 50

URHAN
History and Archaeology

The Landleague

There was a house in Scrahan called the Landleague House. It was built in one day. There were two hundred horses working there. The stones they built it with were like brick. It was a thatch bothán. There were three windows overhead. They had a band and they played it when the house was finished. It happened about 78 years ago. It was burned down a few nights afterwards.

Collector: Peadar Ó hÚrdail, Eyeries, Co. Cork

The Landleague field

William Dwyer lived above near the hill in a little thatch house. When Payne was an agent by Landlord White, he used to come up to Castletownbere taking the rent. There were two men going around the country telling the people not to pay the rent. Their names were Charles Parnell and Michael Davitt. Then many people followed them. William Dwyer was one that did not pay, also Paddy Cait, Mickey Fada and many more. When Payne saw that some of the tenants were not paying, he evicted them. There is a little bit of land between the road and the Landleague field and William Dwyer came down and built a hut there. Then he asked the neighbours to build a house for him and they did. Then he made a settlement and Payne let him live in his own house again above. The house that William Dwyer built below was called the Landleague house and then people called the field the Landleague field.

Collector: Seán Ó Súilleabháin, Coulagh, Co. Cork

The Cillíneach

There is a Cillíneach in Coulagh. It is said that there was a church there and a priest. It was not a big church but a small low one. It is said that it was a stone altar that was in it. There were big stones one on top of the other. There were not many windows in it. The kind of windows that were in it were holes in the walls. Some of the seats were made of timber and some of stones thrown on top of each other.

Collector: Seán Ó Néill, Coulagh, Co. Cork
Informant: Bríghid Ní Néill, Grandparent

There is a field in Ahabrock belonging to Daniel Harrington. The name of it is Gort a' Cillínig. There was a Cillíneach there long ago. There were many people buried there during the time of the famine. There are many golláns standing in it. The bean sidhe was heard there several times.

Collector: Domhnal Ó Súilleabháin, Kilcatherine, Co. Cork

There is a Cillíneach in our field in Cahirkeem. It was consecrated in the olden times. There are not any grown up people buried there now only children. There is a ruin of a church there. There was a church there long ago and the ruin only is there now. If any people would be sick, they used to make rounds around the Cillíneach.

Collector: Seosaimh Ó Mhurchadha, Caherkeen, Co. Cork

There was a Church in Coulagh and there were many monks in it. It is now used as a Cillíneach. In the time of the famine there were many people buried there without coffins.

Collector: Pádruig Ó Cróinín, Coulagh, Co. Cork
Informant: Micheál Ó Cróinín

Carraigreacha an Aifrinn - Tig an tSagairt

Tig an t-Sagairt is a rock in which the Priests used to say Mass long ago. They used to go hide from the English and they used to say Mass there. There is a rock facing west and there is another one near it. The Priest used to stand on that rock, and he used to keep things on the other rock. Then there is another rock facing out from them. The people used to kneel all around. There is a sign of a horse's shoe on the rock.

Collector: Pádruig Ó Ceallaigh, Caherkeen, Co. Cork

Cnocán an Aifrinn

There is a Cnocán in the top of John Kelly's Leact named Cnocán an Aifrinn. It is supposed that it was used as a place for saying mass by the priests long ago in the time of the Penal Days. There is a well above it and it never dried, and it is said that it was blessed by the priests that time. One day Mike Sheehan was cutting turf above it, and he found a piece of a blessed candle. It is supposed that it was a blessed candle the priests had. Fr Casey, P.P., has that bit of candle now.

Collector: Diarmuid Ó Dubhgáin, Caherkeen, Co. Cork

Hedge Schools

There was a hedge-school in Ahabrock in a small garden belonging to Dan Sullivan. They used to cut long scalps and leave them dry well. They used to build a small wall and they used put the scalps on the top of it. That was the seat they had. The roof they had was made of rods. The turf they had was called móin uaite. The writing pens they had were quills. The books they had were called Sequel No. 1. They used a turnip as the map of the world. There was a Hedge-school in Eyeries also.

Collector: Peadar Ó hÚrdail, Eyeries, Co. Cork

Schools

There was an old school in Coulagh long ago. The name of the teacher was Baitín Dubh. He was not left long teaching there because he was transferred to another school. Another teacher came in his place. His name was Justin MacCarthy. He was teaching for a long time in the old school in Urhan. It is now used as a cowhouse. The kind of desks they used to have were made of stones, and every morning when the pupils used to go to school they had to bring in a stone each of them to sit on it. They used not speak anything in it but Irish.

Collector: Padruig Ó Cróinín, Coulagh, Co. Cork
Informant: Micheál Ó Cróinín

Na Scoláirí Bochta

Long ago there were not any schools but one here and there. There were not any teachers also, but strange learned men used to go around the place to teach the children. These teachers were called na scoláirí bochta. They used not ask any money from the people but lodging and food. When they came first, they used to teach to all the children together. They would give a week or a month in every house teaching to the children. Some of the people were poor and so they used not keep them in the night at all. They would keep them and feed them in the day. The teachers used to teach them all about the stars, the signs of the weather. They used to have a little history and geography and a little reading also. They used to have slates and slate pencils. Everything used to be written on the slates.

One night there was one of these teachers teaching in a house. When the time was up the teacher went to the door to go out and he said something when he was going out, but they did not understand him. He was not long out when he returned, and he said to the man of the house that he saw a strange thing in the sky. The man was trying to find out what he meant but the teacher did not tell him for some time. At last, he told the man, he said that he saw a cross in one of the stars in the sky and he said that was a bad sign for one of his daughters. He said that his daughter was going to steal everything that would come before her.

Collector: Pádruig Ó Síothcháin, Caherkeen, Co. Cork
Informant: Máire Ní Shíothcháin, Grandparent

Tales of Líoses

There is a líos in our Gáirdín 'a Cathrach. It is said that the steps leading into it are starting near the gable of Goggin's old house. It is said that two men went into it long ago and they brought with them a candle and a line and while they were going in, they were stretching the line along the ground. When they went down a few steps they lit their candle and when they were halfway in their candle went out on account of the bad air. They did not know how to come out, so they caught the line, and they made their way out with the line. It is said that it was a hiding place for the people long ago during the time of the Danes.

Collector: Diarmuid Ó Dúbhgáin, Caherkeen, Co. Cork
Informant: Séamus Ó Dúbhgáin

A líos is a place where fairies used to live long ago. During the time of the Black and Tans the men used to go in there hiding from the soldiers. The following story happened about forty years ago. One morning as a man was minding his cows near a líos, he saw a strange man near him, and he asked him could he come with him for a while. The man told him that he would not that he would have to mind his cows from the potatoes that grew in the field. The man told him to come on with him that he would not delay him long, that the cows would not touch the plants. The man went with him, and he brought him into the líos. When he went in there was a crowd of people inside and a priest. They asked him would he stand up to a baby and he said he would. The child was baptised and after a while the men asked him what present would he give the child and he said he had not anything to give her. They said to give her the calf that the red cow in the field was going to have. The man said alright, and he went back to the field and the cows were there and they did not go near the potatoes. The man went home with the cows, and he never told his wife what happened. The cow calved and the calf she had was a heifer. When she was three years old, she was going to calf and one evening.

When the man went for the cows, he found her dead in the field. When the wife heard it, she was very sorry, and the man told her that the calf did not belong to himself that he belonged to a baby that he stood up for. The wife never knew what happened until then.

Collector: Seosaimh Ó Mhurchadha, Caherkeen, Co. Cork

Stories of the Famine

Around the time of the famine the people were very poor. There were too many people, and the farms were too small to make any good living. The gardens they used set were small. In the year 1845 the potatoes blackened so they had hardly anything else to eat so the famine followed. They used get up with the sun and go out working right away. They used to have no breakfast before they used to go out. The women used get ready whatever they used to have for their breakfast. Then the men used come in about ten o' clock and eat. Away they used to go again working and stay working until late in the evening. Once there was a man going home from work and as he was going in the door he fell and died.

The houses they had that time were all thatched. There were no cement floors. Some people used to have the cows and horse in the house. Others used to have them outside but when a cow would be about to calf they used to bring her in and tie her to the leg of the seat. When the cows used calf, the houses used be in an mess in the morning.

It is said that there is a man buried above Árd na Ceárdchan. He died in the time of the famine where he is now buried. There is a stone where he is buried. Crowds used be buried in the Cillíneach. The people used dig holes in the ground and throw the corpses into them without any coffins. Any people that had turnips they used eat them. Any people that had not they used die in the side of the road or in the fields.

Collector: Seán Ó Néill, Coulagh, Co. Cork
Informant: Bríghid Ní Néill

Long ago in the time of the famine there was a man living in Coulagh. His name was Patrick Shea. He lived west from our house. He was very poor for he had no farm. He had three daughters and a son. The three daughters died of the hunger. The father and the son dug a grave, before the grave was dug the son died, and the father put the four into the one grave, and he himself lay down beside the grave and died.

Collector: Seán Ó Súilleabháin, Coulagh, Co. Cork
Informant: Seán Ó Súilleabháin

The Famine started in the year 1845. The people were very poor. The people that had turnips used to eat them and other people used boil nettles and put a drop of milk through them. The English used not give any food to them. There was a woman in Coulagh named Maire Ní Leamhna. Her son died and she had no one to bury him. He was dead in the house for three days. She used be looking at the Cillíneach to see if anyone would be burying people there. One day she saw a funeral below and she put the boy across her shoulder and brought him down and they buried him. They used shake hay down on the body and then throw earth down on that. There was a man buried in the Comar to the west of our house. He was taking a rest there, and he died there, and he was buried where he died. His grave is still to be seen there. There were two men going around with a horse and cart. They used bury the dead people.

Collector: Diarmuid Ó Cróinín, Coulagh, Co. Cork
Informant: Mícheál Ó Cróinín

EYERIES

Co. Chorcaighe
Bar: Béara
Par: Cill Choitairainn
Scoil: Na Haodhraí
Oide: Proinnsias Ó Hurdail

Eyeries
Local Folklore and Stories

Mic Eóghan's Treasure

Many years ago, a man named Mic Eóghan served in the army for the King of France. He was exceedingly rich and was a great friend of the king. It happened that the king had a very pretty daughter and Mic Eóghan wanted to marry her. The king would not consent to their marriage, so he and the princess fled from France. When the king heard that his daughter left, he ordered his men to follow Mic Eóghan. They saw him after they reached Ireland. Mic Eóghan then turned to the direction of Berehaven and the others never saw him afterwards. When he was dying, he buried his riches in a place which can be seen today. It is said to be hidden in a stone wall which surrounds an old burial ground. Efforts were made to discover the treasure, but they proved fruitless.

A Young Man from Inches

Long ago, many fairies used to be seen in this part of the country. If they caught any people out after dark, they would take them and question them, and if they would not answer the questions which would be put to them, they would punish them. A young man from Inches was not afraid of them, so he used to go for a walk every evening. One evening as he was going for a walk, he met three men who were carrying a coffin on their shoulders. He went under the coffin to help the men, but while he was looking around the fairies disappeared. He took the coffin from his shoulder and opened it. He found a young girl with rings on her mouth and hands. He took her out and brought her home to her mother, as only her mother was with her in her home. Next day she told them all what had happened to her.

Crossroads

There are many stories about crossing paths in the night-time. Long ago it was very dangerous to pass one during the night as it was said that the fairies used to be seen there. One night a boy was going west to Urhan. The night was very dark, and he was in a hurry, so he went by a short cut. When he was going out on the road a man came out of a bush and gave the boy a slap across the head. When he went home, he was very pale. The sign of a hand was marked across his head.

A Strange Light

One night a man from this district was going on a journey on horseback. He also had a dog with him. After about going two or three hundred yards, he saw a light before him. He was greatly afraid as the light kept going on before him. When he had gone about a mile, he saw that the light had stopped. When he reached it, he saw that it was a lantern hanging on a cow's horn. The horse was frightened and threw the man from his back and ran away very quickly. The dog started to cry and ran off in a great fright. The man never saw his horse or dog again. He was afterwards called Sean Spriod.

The Ghostly Priest

Long ago a woman lived in Coulagh. She had four sons and they were altar clerks. One day their mother went to town, and she stayed there that night. About one o'clock in the night the woman awoke, and she called the people of the house, and told them to get up that it was morning. They told her to remain in bed, but afterwards they let her go out. When she was about a mile and a half from the town, she saw a man who was dressed in black walking before her. He was reading a book. She walked quickly and when she got up to him, she said good morning. He said that it was time for the living to be resting and the dead to be working. Then he told her that long ago he was a priest in the Eyeries parish, and he got money to say Mass for some person, but he did not say it. He also told her to tell he eldest son to go over to the church the next night at twelve o'clock to answer Mass for him. The next day the four boys were going to the mines, and their mother told the oldest boy to stay at home. She told the second and third and they said they would not. Then she told the youngest boy to remain at home and he said that he would. That night he went to the church and when he went in the candles were lit and the priest was on the altar. When he had answered Mass, he went home. The next day the other three boys were killed in the Mines.

EYERIES
People, Places and Property

Peg Murphy

A woman lived in Kilcatherine long ago whose name was Peg Murphy. She earned her living by selling eggs as most people did at that time. She used to travel to towns far and near and sell her eggs. One Summer's morning at about three o clock this woman started on her journey to Cork. She carried a basket of eggs on her back. After two days she returned home again. She had walked to Cork and back again during that time.

Seán Dubh

Long ago, a man lived near Eyeries Village whose name was Seán Dubh. Nail making was his way of living. One day, as he was sitting outside his door making nails, he noticed a man coming towards him. As the man drew near to Sean, he spoke to him. After a long conversation Seán decided to keep him for that night. During the night an argument arose between the men, and they began to fight. As soon as the man caught Seán he turned black and that was the reason why he was called Seán Dubh.

Cahirkeem

Many local places got their names from brave warriors who lived long ago. Cahirkeem got its name from a man whose name was Cathal an Chaoin. One morning during the spring months, Cathal an Chaoin prepared for a duel. He met his enemy at Cahirkeem, and they both fought bravely. After a fierce battle Cathal an Chaoin was killed. His opponent died shortly afterwards from wounds which he received. Both were buried at Cahirkeem At the present day the place where they were buried is marked by two stones.

Fords

There are many fords in this place where people used to cross for shortcuts when the war was in Ireland. There is one in the river that flows below the village of Eyeries. It was found by two men who thought it was a good plan to cross there instead of going around roads as there were not any bridges at that time. It was found during the time when the war was in Ireland, and it was also leading to a good hiding place for the Irish to hide in. It is now very hard to find it as it is a long time since anybody passed there.

Eyeries
Farming, Trade and Crafts

Foxes

The fox was first brought to Castletownbere by a man who lived with O'Sullivan Bere. His name was Feóras. It is said that he was spending a holiday in some part of Ireland. When he returned home, he brought three young foxes to Castletownbere. When he arrived, he left them on the strand. He went back to the ship, and when he came to the shore again the foxes were gone. They killed many hens during the night. Feóras meant to keep the foxes as pets, and never thought they would do damage in the place.

The Wicked Man

Long ago there lived in Kerry a very wealthy man. He was very old, and he knew he was soon going to die but he did not want to give his money to anybody. His brother was a very wicked man. He killed several people to get money, and he wanted to do the same to his brother. Before the man died, he put his money under a stone on a riverbank. One night the man died and there was nobody with him only the wicked man. The wicked man tried everywhere for the money, but he could not find it. He wished to get the money and he prayed to the devil to tell him where the money was. One night the devil appeared to him and led him to the riverbank. He told him to take up the stone and that he would find the money. He was just about to rise the stone when suddenly he found himself in the middle of a fire. This fire was hell. The devil had thrown him into hell because he committed many sins during his life. He prayed to the devil when he wished to get anything.

Eyeries
Local Customs

Killcatherine Holy Well

There is much tradition connected with wells in this district. The people believe that these wells have power to cure people of certain diseases. One of these wells is in Kilcatherine. The people of this district say that a girl lived there once. She got very ill with measles and nothing could cure her. Her father was one day thinking of what he could do to save his daughter, when suddenly he remembered that there was a holy well not far from his house. He went at once to get the water, as he was afraid his daughter might die quickly. When he returned with the water, he found out that his daughter was dying. He gave her some of the water to drink and it instantly cured her.

Old Customs

In olden times many strong healthy people lived in this parish. There were no motorcars in the district at that time and the people used to travel from place to place in sidecars. It was the custom to walk long distances to get a good price for butter and eggs. The people of this parish were accustomed to walk to Cork and would often start on their journey in the morning and would be back on the following evening. They used take off their shoes and walk barefooted until they came near the town or city and would then put on their shoes. When they had their butter and eggs sold, they would leave the city and return home without any food.

EYERIES
Sea and Shipwrecks

Drowning

About fifty or sixty years ago, seven men went out to fish near the coast. They were preparing to return to the shore when a storm arose. They struggled on for some time, but after a while a large wave washed four of the men overboard. The others could do nothing to save their lives and were driven from place to place with the force of the high waves and strong wind. When the storm ceased, only two fishermen reached the shore. One of them died shortly afterwards. The other who was a native of Foromanes was the only man who lived. Deep was the sorrow of the relatives and neighbours of the surrounding district when they heard of the sad tragedy which occurred. The people spent some days searching for the bodies of the fishermen who were drowned, and they were found about a week afterwards.

In the year 1918 a most striking incident occurred in Ballycrovane Harbour where the lives of four were lost. It happened that two seine boats were returning from their nights fishing, each boat bearing a crew of nine. It seems that they were racing and unfortunately one boat was pitched on a rock. Immediately the boat turned but by the aid of the other crew five were saved. The other four were drowned instantly.

EYERIES
History and Archaeology

A Líos

There is a large líos in Boffichil. As the years passed by the entrance closed gradually. Many people went into it, and it is said that rooms and seats are carved in stone. Six men went into it one day. They had a candle. They were not long inside when the candle was quenched. They had not matches nor any other light so they were in darkness. They tried to get out, but it was in vain. After some time, they started the rosary. When it was said they found their way out again. Any person did not go in after that event.

Ancient Paths

In ancient times paths or shortcuts, as they used to be called, were numerous in this parish. When coming home from a village or town, people used to go through the shortcuts so as to reach home quickly. In later years people built houses on some of the paths and prevented the people from passing in that direction. A man who lived in this parish prevented the people from going through the path by building a fence at the end. Each night afterwards when the people of that house went to bed, they could not sleep as great noise was heard and people were seen in the rooms. After a time, the man told a priest of his experiences as he thought his house was enchanted. Early next morning the priest arrived at the house and celebrated Mass. He also told the man to remove the fence which he had built at the end of the lane. He did as he was told instantly, and nothing was seen afterwards. It is believed that an old woman who lived in the house long ago haunted it.

KILMACKOWEN

Co. Chorcaighe
Bar: Béara
Par: Cill Choitiarainn
Scoil: Cill Mhic Eoghain
Oide: Domhnall Ó Hurdail

KILMACKOWEN
Local Folklore and Stories

Comhla Bhreac

Long ago the priests were not allowed to say Mass. One morning a priest was saying Mass on a rock called the Comhla Bhreach when a soldier came from the east on horse-back. The priest did not see the soldier, and he killed the priest. The rock bent in the form of a church door and the blood still remains on the rock. The soldiers got killed also.

Collector: Mary Harrington,
Informant: Ellen Harrington, Kilcatherine

Once there was a widow from the western parish and her son was a priest. One Sunday the priest was saying Mass in the Kilineach for the people, and there was an English soldier amongst the people, who was hired by Cromwell for beheading priests. Cromwell gave £5 for each priest's head and when Mass was over the soldier went out with the people. He waited outside until all the people were gone home. Then he went back into the Church and beheaded the priest. He brought it to Cromwell in Dunboy, and when the priest's mother heard, she prayed before breakfast the following morning that the eagles would devour the body of the man who killed her son. Very early next morning he was coming along Beal na Lapa on horse-back, he heard a man coughing up among the rocks on the roadside. He looked up and saw it was a priest. He could not reach the rock where the priest was standing. He stole up around at the back to kill him, and as he leaned back over the rock with his sword, the rock leaned back, the horseman over balanced, and fell to the ground on top of a stone and was made in pieces. He was devoured by the eagles which nested in the hill in which the Comhla Bhreach is situated, namely Cnoc an Fholair.

Collector: Mary Harrington, Bawnard, Co. Cork
Informant: Dan Murphy, aged 90, Gowlane

Carraig Fhíll

Long ago there was a man going around the district who did many misdeeds. One day he went to Urhan and did some misdeeds. The people sent word to him and said they would forgive him his deeds if he went out to a rock about a mile outside Urhan. He did it, and the people followed him out. When he was as far as the rock, they cut off his head, and threw it into the sea. A few days after that it came into a strand about a mile east the rock. The natives put it up on a spike warning the other people not to do the same treachery. That place is now called Árd a Chloigeann. Chloigeann is called after the head. About a week after that the body came into a strand about a half a mile inside the rock. That place is now called Cathair Cúin, and in English Cahirkeem. Carraig Fhíll is called after the treachery that was done there.

Collector: Mary O'Neil, Kilmackowen, Co. Cork

Holy Wells - Réidh Fhineáin

Long ago St Finnian and another saint were out boating in the Kenmare River, and a British Man of War came along. The two saints came into the land to preach to the people, and the owner of the Man of War stole their boat. When they came back to where they left it, they saw it tied on to the Man of War, and they followed it by land around the coast. The Man of War came in near Kilcatherine, and the two saints followed it until they came to Réidh Fineáin. When they came to that place they lost sight of the boats, and one of the saints gave a kick to the ground with his shoe, and he said, "my curse on this place." As he was saying these words a well opened under his feet. A few yards away from this place St Finnian gave another kick to the ground with his shoe and he said, "my blessing on this place and the curing for man and beasts." Then he said, "my curse on the rushes." As he was saying this a well opened under his feet. The old people say that since St Finnian put this curse on the rushes that their tops are never seen green. This happened in May Eve and still people go to this place and make rounds as they are called there.

Collector: Ann McAuliffe
Informant: Michael McAuliffe, Crumpane

Maire Eóghain

The old people can tell several fairy stories yet. A very old woman named Maire Eóghain lived in William Power's old house near the hill long ago. She used go to town very often. One evening as she was coming home, she was taken away near Castletown Bere by fairies, and she came back the next day again. She got very sick after this, and Julia Hanley was gathering furze in the hill one day, and she went down to see her. Máire Eóghain stood in the door and she looked up at the hill, and said it was very lonesome. Then she asked who cut the furze, and Julia Hanley said, "it is my husband Paddy Hanley." Máire Eóghain said you will not have him long more. After this Paddy Hanley died. The old woman knew always when people were to die. This old house is about three miles from Castletown Bere, in the parish of Eyeries.

Collector: Sheila Hanley, Bawnard, Co. Cork
Informant: Julia Hanley, grandmother, aged 75

Daniel Kelly on the Clash Road

One night about four years ago, there was a man visiting one of his neighbours' houses. His name is Daniel Kelly. When he was coming home it was about one o'clock. He went up the Clash Road as it was the shortest way for him to go home. There is one part of the road where there are trees growing. When he was passing them, someone came out of the bushes and caught him. He was dragged into the river. He could not see anybody, but when he was trying to go away, he found he was caught tightly. After a while he was left go and when he tried to walk, he was not able. He crept a few yards and then he was able to walk. It was four o'clock when he reached home. He went to bed and did not get up for a week.

Collector: Claire McAuliffe, Eyeries, Co. Cork
Informant: Michael McAuliffe

KILMACKOWEN
People, Places and Property

Landlords

There were several landlords in this part of Ireland long ago, but they were not all here at the same time. Some of them were very cruel, and the people set no value on them, but other landlords were not so bad. Many farmers were evicted from their land and possessions, and then they were very poor. The old people tell us several stories about evictions, and about people who were evicted, because they didn't pay the rent. Our farm is situated in Shountalive which is about three miles to the east of Eyeries. It contains about twenty-five acres of land, and long ago my grandfather kept nine cows in it, but now we have only seven. The rent was £20, but like all the other farmers, my grandfather entered the Land Court in order to reduce the rent. At first it was brought down to £18, and they paid this sum for three years. Then they entered the Land Court again and brought it down to £15. In this way rent was reduced to £3. In the time when my grandfather was young, it was very hard for the people to make up the rent. It was all they worked and lived for; and sometimes they used have to borrow it from their neighbours. The cows were fed very well, and it was with nettles or meal the people fed them. Then the people made a lot of butter and sold it for the rent.

There were only two landlords in this parish namely Lord Aurdalaun and Lord Bantry. Lord Aurdalaun owned Goulane and Kilmackowen and Lord Bantry owned all the other villages. Each of these landlords had agents who gathered the rents for them. Lord Aurdalauns agent was Carroll Leahy and Lord Bantry's was Mr Payne. They had an office in Castletown, and the people went in there to pay them. They paid the rent in March, and September, and if they did not, the agents came to the house for it. David Donovan, and Daniel Kelly from Baurs used to go around and give them notice to pay the rent.

Collector: Sheila Hanley, Bawnard, Co. Cork
Informant: Tim Hanley, aged 52

The farm we have at present was owned by my grandfather about sixty years ago. It contained forty acres of land, and kept ten cows, and we only keep seven at present. The rent was twenty pounds. They worked very hard to get that rent. Lord Bantry was the landlord over our farm and his agent was Mr Ellis. Lord Bantry did not live in this parish at all. He had a house in Bantry. His name was Mr Leigh White He was not a very good Landlord at all. They paid the rent on March and September. Mr Ellis did not accept half rents at all. One time my grandfather could not pay the full rent and Mr Ellis would not take it from him. A few days after that, he was threatened with eviction. He borrowed the money from Kevin Sullivan's grandfather. He got it from him, and paid it, and he was not evicted after all. They were paying twenty pounds for eight years. At the time of the Land League, he entered the land court. It was reduced to eighteen pounds then. They paid that amount for six years. Then he entered the land-court again. It was reduced to fourteen pounds, and they paid fourteen pounds for five years. He entered the Land Court again and it was reduced to what it is at present.

Collector: Clair MacAuliffe, Crumpane, Co. Cork
Informant: Michael MacAuliffe, aged 56

My grandfather's name was Tim Sullivan. He lived in Carrig, about a mile from the Kilmacowen school. He had a farm of twenty acres, and he had five cows. The landlord who owned his farm, was Lord Bantry. He was a bad man. One time my grandfather had not the rent. When the landlord came around for the rent my grandfather handed him all he had. Lord Bantry said that would not do. If he wouldn't give it to him now he would be evicted. My grandfather then borrowed it from his next door neighbour, and he gave it to the landlord. There were two special months of the year, March and September. The people used go to town in crowds, and they used stand outside the office, and the landlord used come out, and if he would see any friend of his among the crowd he would call him in. Sometimes people would be there for days before the rent used be paid. Sometimes the people used go to Cork, and they used have a jolly time of it. They had very little sleep. One time a man went to Cork, and he missed his companion, and the first man he met he asked him did he see Jack Barry.

Collector: Peg Sullivan, Carrig, Co. Cork
Informant: Gerry Sullivan, aged 50

Landlords long ago were very plentiful. My grandfather's name was Patrick Hanley, and he had a very big farm. It consisted of eighteen acres of land. He was paying sixteen pounds rent twice a year. It used be paid in March and September. It came down then to three pounds, and now my father is paying that amount. It was Lord Bantry that owned my grandfather's farm. He was not a very good man at all. My grandfather was going to be evicted one year long ago, but he got a chance. He went to town three times before he could pay it. They first time he went he could not pay it because he had only half the money. The next day he went, he was late. The next day he went, and he paid it.

Collector: Anna Hanley, Bawnard, Co. Cork
Informant: Tim Hanley, aged 50

About sixty years ago, our farm was owned by Lord Aurdalaun. It contains about thirty acres of Land, and the rent was sixteen pounds. My grandfather entered the Land Court three times, and they brought it down to two pounds. My grandfather was threatened with eviction. He went to town and paid half of the rent to the agent, Caroll Leahy. The agent took it, but he was to pay the other half within a week. My grandfather borrowed the money and paid it next day. Carroll Leahy was a good agent. He was considerate towards his tenants. Sometimes he used pay the rent for them and he used give them a month to pay it back to himself. My grandmother used go out every morning at five o'clock, and cut nettles for the cows. In the evening she used pull green grass off the fences after being working hard all day. But they had to do those things in order to pay the rent. The young children used mind the cows around the potato field, and near the rye grass.

Collector: Eileen Murphy, Gowlane, Co. Cork
Informant: Patrick Murphy, aged 57

Graveyards

There are several small graveyards in this parish, but some of them are very small and they are not very important. Some of them are not used now except very seldom. The small ones are called Cíllíeachs, and there are several of them in this parish. There is one of these Cíllíneacs situated about half a mile north from this school, and there are several stories told about it. It is very old and nobody around this part of the parish knows when it was first used. It is not very big, and there is a stone wall or fence all round it. There are no trees or flowers growing in it, only grass. There are old ruins to be seen. There was a church there long ago. It is not known when this church was made, or when it was last used. There were several grown-up people buried in this Cíllíneach during the time of the famine and before it. There were no people buried in it since then, and now it is used only as a child's graveyard. There are no headstones in this Cillíneach as there are in others. There is a stone cross standing up in the middle of the field and it is said that this was erected there in memory of MacEóghain's wife who is buried there. There was writing on the cross, but it cannot be made out now.

There is a graveyard in Kilcatherine, and the people are buried in it still. It is very old now, and there are ruins of an old church to be seen near it. Long ago there were no headstones in this graveyard, and the first one was put there in memory of Marcus Óg who was the last of the O'Sullivans.

Old Roads

L ong ago there were not many good roads in Ireland. There were several of them made in the time of the famine as an excuse for getting relief meal.

There were several old paths leading across hills, which were very useful as short-cuts. They were very useful when the people were going to mass because they had no other roads. The fences which were on each side of these paths are still to be seen in some places, but they are very few. There was one road leading from Kilmackowen to Ardgroom, and it was most useful. It was going north across a hill called Mullach and was passing near Bawer's wood. The people of this parish went through it when they were going to the wood for timber. This road was very useful, because there was a bog near it, and the people drew their turf through it. There was an old road from Castletown to Eyeries, and it was called Bothar Dubh. It received this name because the ground through which it was made is black and boggy. In some places it is very bad and narrow, and it is being repaired at present. This was the main road long ago, but there was a new road made in the time of the famine. The people who worked in this road got free meal because they had nothing else to eat, and even a few of them died with hunger and weakness.

The road going from Castletown to Eyeries was made in the time of the famine. The road, which was made before that, was very narrow, and broken. It extended from Castletown to Pullincha bridge, then it went as far as Richard Donovan's house. It passed Clash River, and there was a bridge going across it, but it is not to be seen now. The place where the bridge was, is still called The old bridge, and the field near it is called Páirc an Droichid. Very few people go this road now, and for that reason there is grass growing on it.

There was an old road going west across the hill from Banard to Eyeries long ago. The old people used draw weeds up from the strand on horseback through this road long ago. This is a great near way at present because they go to Mass through it. Before the Urhan road was made there was an old road coming as far as Eyeries. This road is very bad. Some of the Urhan people come to Mass through it at present

Ár gCeantar Féin

The name of my district is Croumhane. There are seventeen houses in this townland. Some of these houses are thatched and others are slated. These houses are neatly kept and whitewashed inside and outside. They are all farmers houses. The land is fairly poor and for that reason the farmers work hard at their crops and all sorts of outdoor work. There is a big river running through this district. This river is called the Kilmackowen river. It is the longest river in this parish. There are nice trees growing near the bank of this river. We have thirty four acres of land in our farm. We have one acre of land under potatoes and another under oats. We have the rest under hay and grass for the cows. We have bogs in our farm. There is very good turf in this bog.

Collector: Dick Donovan, Crumpane, Co. Cork

Shountalive

The name of my village is Shountalive. It consists of only two houses but long ago there were three of them there. There are two or three old ruins to be seen. The dwelling-houses are kept very neat. Shountalive is in the townland of Kilmacowen as it is too small to be a townland in itself. Shountalive is in the parish of Eyeries which long ago was called the parish of Kilcatherine. There is a small river separating it from Goulane. It does not flow to the sea as it joins the Kilmacowen river and stones are taken out of it for building houses or cabins. In this school district the population is about three hundred. There are about five people in every house, and there are about sixty houses. There are seventy-eight children in school, and there are about twenty-four people who are over seventy years of age. Most of these old people speak English but there are three or four of them who can speak Irish. Very few of them can tell stories in Irish language, but they do when the children ask them.

Emigration is closed for the past fourteen years, but while it was open several people from this school district went to America. When the oldest of the family was nineteen or twenty years, he emigrated to America. If he had any friend there, he went to them, and they had a job ready for him. When he was earning money in America for a few years, he sent the passage money to the next member of the family. In this way all the family emigrated except one boy who stayed at home to take care of his parents and the farm. For the past seven or eight years, the young boys and girls of Ireland emigrate to England, and very few of them can go to America. They earn a lot of money and send some of it home to their parents for Christmas. They come home for a holiday in the Summer or at Christmas, and they enjoy this very well as most of them have to work very hard in England.

Collector: Mary Murphy, Gowlane, Co. Cork
Informant: Mrs Annie Murphy, aged 89

Carrig

I am living in a small place called Carrig. It is in the townland of Kilmacowen. There are four houses in this place. Carrig is a very high rocky place and some of the land is very wild. The land in Maulin is very coarse, and cattle do not feed there. You would see in the bottom of a hill where gardens were set. There is an old cabhlach in the bottom of the hill in our field. Long ago, in the time of the famine, the man of the house died with hunger. He went outside the door, and he fell. He was buried in the same place with a sheet around him. Every Summer beautiful roses grow where he was buried.

Collector: Peg Sullivan, Carrig, Co. Cork
Informant: Gerry Sullivan, aged 50

Kilmackowen
Farming, Trade and Crafts

Farm Animals

The names of our cows are Kerry, Purty, Leath h-adharc, Crón, Lily, and Daisy. When we are driving them home, we say "Habha abhaile." When we drive them out of the cowhouse we say, "habha amach." Long ago we used cut furze with a geárrthóir for the cows. We used put through the furze, meal, oats and bran. It was called a bribe when it was given to them before milking.

The horse was fed very well long ago, because they won several races. They used get oats, potatoes and corn. Boiled eggs were given to them before a race. Working horses were fed in a different way. Furze was the usual food given to the horse. Long ago people had no furze-machine, and it was a gearrthóir. A hole was dug in the ground called an umar. The furze was put into the umar and bruised with a sharp iron with a knife on the bottom of it.

Collector: Dick Donovan, Crumpane, Co. Cork
Informant: Mrs Richard Donovan, aged 50

Cows

We have eight cows in our farm, and each of them has a name. Their names are Blackeen, Kerry, Reddy, Starry, Cronie, Cuby, Culie and Bánie. Most of them are called after their colours or the way their horns are shaped. The food which the cows got was hay oats and sometimes ground furze. If they were fattening a cow, they would cut hay and put it into tubs or boxes. Then we shake meal on the hay, and scald it with a kettle of boiling water. It is given to the cow every morning and evening. Every night the cows are tied with what we call a neasg. These are tied around their horns in a way that they could not loosen. The calves and young heifers are tied around the neck with what is called a bragh dhán. When a cow jumps over ditches and does damage in other people's fields we put a cruith-neasc on her. This ties her horns to her front leg so that then she can walk but very slowly. When a cow is cross while milking her, we put a spancel on her, which keeps her quiet

Collector: Mary Murphy, Kilmackowen, Co. Cork
Informant: Mrs Dennis Sullivan, aged 73

The Churn

Long ago the people in this parish used make butter different to what they do now. Long ago they had no tin pans. They had coolers and they used call them keelers. The keelers were made of timber. They were very useful, but it was hard to wash them. They were to be scalded out three or four times before the milk used be put into them.

My grandmother told me several piseogs about churning. Long ago the people were very superstitious. They believed in several piseogs. It is not right to go into a house in which a churn is being made without twisting, or striking it. It is not right to smoke in a house in which a churn is being made. Sometimes if the churn would not make, the people would sprinkle holy water on it to bless it. The old people were very careful while making the churn. Each person struck the churn in his turn. If the cream was cold, they put hot water in it, and then it was not long making. After a while the churn would begin to change or to break. They knew not to go into a house in which a churn is being made without twisting or striking it. It is not right to smoke in a house in which a churn is being made. There was a spile in the bottom of the cream tub. This spile was used when the tub was full. The spile was a wooden peg that was put on a hole in the bottom of the tub. The milk in the bottom of the tub used be taken out through the spile. There was a round ring made of rods around the staff near the cover to keep down the cream. They used bring the rods to the church every Palm Sunday to be blessed before being put on the churn. These rods were made in the shape of a cup, but there was no bottom in them, because the staff was put up through it.

Long ago, when the people used make butter, one person from the parish used go to Cork and bring it with him. It used take them three days to go and three days to come, and they used stay a night in Cork. They used buy several things for the people who sent butter there. They used stop at certain places along their way. There is a story told about a man who was going to Cork with a load of butter. He was gone over half the journey when his horse took head and he stopped near a public house where his master used always stop. The churns in olden times were different from the churn at the present days.

We have an old churn at home still. This churn is very large. It is very wide in the bottom, and it is getting narrow as it comes towards the top. The top of it is made of tin. We have a churn staff is made of wood. It is a very long handle and there is a round flat piece of wood at the bottom. There is a wooden cover for this churn and the middle and it is stuck into the churn staff.

Informant: Michael Harrington, Kilmackowen

Trade in Olden Days

There are several old trades in this parish. The old people used make several useful things such as candles, thread, nails and other things. Spinning is very common in this parish. My grandmother Julia Hanley is very good at this trade. Sometimes she spins for some of the neighbours. She lives in Bawnard, about a mile north of this school. She has a big wheel resting on a stool. There is a piece of twine around it, and the spindle is in the opposite side of the wheel. The wool is sent to Kenmare to be carded before it is spun, and long ago the people used card it for themselves.

The old people used make their own candles long ago. Whenever they killed a cow, the tallow was kept and melted. Every house had moulds. They were placed point downward on a sod of turf. The wick was passed through it and fastened at the top by a nail. The boiled tallow was poured into the mould then and left to set, and after a few hours it is taken out.

There was a nailer's workshop situated near the village of Eyeries, and some old people say that they remember to see the nailer himself working in it. This man had a very good trade, because there was no other man in this parish who could make nails. He was paid for his work, and there is a place in the village of Eyeries, which is called after him. It is called the Nailer's Height.

Basket-making was a very common trade which the men liked long ago. There were several of them in this parish, but it is said that the man who was best able to do it, was Pat Shanahan who lived in Goulane, which is about three miles to the east of Eyeries. He could make all kinds of baskets, and whenever they were broken, he was a very good hand at mending them. It is to him all the people of the district went when they wanted to make any baskets. His son is the only young man in this district who can make them now, and everybody praises him, because he is very good at this trade.

Long ago the people in this parish bought no ropes, and usually they made them themselves. They could make them as thick or a thin as they liked. There is a man living in Carrig, about a mile to the north of this school who is a good hand at making ropes. His name is Patrick O'Shea and the ropes which he makes last for a long time.

Weaving is another trade we have in this parish. There was a weaver by the name of Timothy Sullivan living in Carrig, about four miles to the north of Castletownbere. He used weave for his neighbours very often and used get paid for his work. His son Jeremiah Sullivan is a weaver, but he does not weave very often.

Long ago the people used have a straw mat against the kitchen door. My father, Daniel Sullivan used make the mats. Sometimes he used make them for the neighbours. The straw used be threshed and cleaned. Then the blades used be gathered together in little bundles. Then the bundles of straw used be traced into one another.

The people long ago used make skiffs for straining potatoes. They were made of rods in the shape of a horseshoe. There used be a strong rod around the edge of the skiff. My brother Edmund Sullivan can make them.

KILMACKOWEN
Leisure

Games

There are several small games played in this part of Ireland, and some of them are very funny. The small games are the nicest and they are played by the children in school, and the home. One very common game which is played in school is "hunting". One person hunts the rest of the girls and boys, and when all of them are caught the game is finished. Then they begin it again by saying:

Ittle, attle black bottle,
Ittle, attle, out goes you.
In the middle of the dark, blue sea.

Sometimes they say another rhyme, which is as follows;-

Ink Pink, penny wink,
All out excepting you.

This is the shortest, and is the handiest, because it need be said only once. Another one is "London bridges broken down". At first two girls catch each other's hands, and each of them chooses something like a golden watch, or a golden chain. Then all the other girls pass under their hands, and while they are doing this, they say this rhyme;

Oranges and lemons,
The bells of our clemons,
We owe you a farthing
And when shall you pay us
Here comes the lighter,
To light you to bed,
And here comes a chopper,
To chop off your head.

Whatever girl is passing when the rhyme is finished is caught and she is asked to choose any of the gifts she likes. Then she goes to the side of the person she chooses, and they keep doing this until the game is finished. When this is done, they all catch hands and pull, and whatever side pulls the farthest has the game. A very common game the children play is "How many miles to Galway. In order to play this game, the children catch hands, and stand in the form of a horse-shoe, and two big girls stand at each end. While they play this game, they say a verse, which is the following:

Q. How many miles to Galway
A. Three score and ten,
Q. Will we be there for candle light
A. Yes, and back again, open the gates and let us in for we're the best of all the men.

While they are saying the latter, the girls lift up their hands, and the ones in the other side push under them. Another very common game is "Old Adam is dead". The children catch each other's hands, and stand in the form of a ring. One girl goes in the ring and closes her eyes while the others say the following:

Old Adam is dead,
And gone to his bed,
This cold and frosty morning.
The apples are ripe,
And ready to fall,
Old Adam get up.
And give us a thump.

When this is said, the girl in the middle stands up and picks out one of the girls in the ring. Then the girl picked out hunts the other one, and she catches her, she goes into the ring and and the same thing is done again. Another game which is very common is "Chicken and Fox". At first a big girl stands in front, and she is supposed to be the mother. Then all the other girls catch each other in a line, and after a while they hear a noise walking around the house, It's supposed to be the fox in there. The fox stands in front of the mother and says as follows:

Q. Whose comes around my story house?
A. Little Daddy fox.
Q. What have you behind your back?
A. A bad of sand.
Q. What do you want the sand for?
A. To brighten the knives
Q. What do you want the knives for?
A. To cut off the chickens' heads
Q. Where are they?
A. Behind your back.

Then the mother is trying to guard her chickens as best she can, while the fox is trying to catch them. According as the fox catch them, he brings them to his den, and he keeps doing that until they are all gone.

Collector: Eileen Murphy, Gowlane, Co. Cork
Informant: Patrick Murphy, aged 57

KILMACKOWEN
Local Customs

Old Houses

The houses in which the people lived long ago were not like the houses which are now to be seen. They were built differently and had several other changes. The houses were not as high or as roomy as they are now. One very big difference was that the houses were all thatched, but they are slated now. There used be only one door on them, and this used be very awkward. They all had half doors, and these were very handy, because they kept out the wind. There used sometimes be only one kitchen, and the window, was a very small one. The whole house contained only two rooms besides the kitchen. They had not enough room for their beds upstairs sometimes, so they put one of them in the kitchen. This bed was closed up during the day and was used as a seat. The floors which they had in the houses long ago were made of earth, and sometimes they had big flags. The lofts were different from the lofts that are there at present. They were called half lofts because they were made in two parts. They had no stairs to go up on these lofts only they used step ladders.

The people long ago kept the hens in the house, and then they had a lot of eggs for sale. The hens were fed in the kitchen, and they were left out every fine day. Whenever a cow or a horse was sick they were brought into the house, and given a nice bed of hay to lie on. The calves were brought into the house when they were young, for fear they would be cold outside.

There was a nice big dresser in the bottom of the kitchen, which was always kept nice and clean. There were lines of jugs hanging on the top of the dresser and down the sides. There were nice dishes on the top of the dresser, and they were used only the day they used have the station. The woman of the house used always have her dresser nice and clean.

The step ladder used be resting on the bottom of the seat. It used be painted blue. The upstairs was very small. There was only one room in it. This bed was nice and clean. There was a bed in this room.

There was always a clean white bed valance hanging from the bottom of the bed to the ground. There was a "clár" [board] at the back of the bed, and the brush for sweeping the rooms was kept there. There was no glass in the windows, but a little door. There were no brushes there at the time, but a little broom made of heather. There was a very big "cleavy" in our old house. It was over the fireplace, and it was stuck into the wall. In some houses this "cleavy" was loose and was easily taken off when necessary. This plank rested on two brackets. Under the "clevy" were two nice crooks fitted into the wall. Clothes were hung on these to dry. They were far better than nails, because they would not tear the clothes. There were two holes near the fire, one at each side. They were very handy for keeping the sáspan of milk warm.

Sean-Nósanna na Marbh

There are several old customs connected with the dying and dead persons of this district. The people of the house always wish to see the dead person look well. When a person dies outside, he is not brought into the house and waked, but he is put to church and buried the next day. The first thing that is done, when a person is dying all the people of the same surname leave the house and go out into an outhouse and a few neighbours are present, to perform the works at the bedside. The eyes and mouth are closed carefully immediately after he draws the last breath. While the person is dying the clock is stopped. Then the people who are present recite the Rosary and the prayers for the dying. Any person does not cry until the corpse is laid out. When he dies, the people who are outside while the death is taking place are called in. Then they start to lay him out. The body is washed and tidied. If the dead person is a man, the face is shaved. Then word is sent to the relatives and friends while another messenger goes for the habit. When the habit arrives, the corpse is dressed in it. They join his hands and put Rosary beads on them. The next day is passed away similarly.

In the evening the coffin is brought. They put a Prayer Book under his head, to keep his mouth closed. If the person is not enrobed in the brown scapular, the best suit he has is put on. Long ago gloves used to be worn, but that custom is dying out at present.

In this place the first thing that is done is to put a door down on the bed, and a white sheet is put down on that. While the women are doing this work, some other person washes the body. Then the face is shaved if he did not wear a beard during his life. Then a habit is put on and the cap of it is hung at the back of the bed. Then a nice clean white cloth is hung from the bottom of the bed to the ground. Long ago a white cloth was placed along the ceiling over the bed and there were crosses of black crape on this. Then the dead person is put into the bed. The hands are placed down by the sides. Long ago the hands were filled with snuff so the people who came to the wake had it to use. In olden days the person was laid out on top of the clothes but for the past ten years or so, the bed clothes are put up as far as the waist. A small table is put near the bed with lit candle on it. Then they prepare for the wake.

A person nearby goes for the things needed for the wake such as pipes, tobacco, snuff, white bread, jam and tea. Then two messengers are sent for stools. When the corpse is laid out, the relatives go into the room and start an ologón. Sometimes the children start to cry before the body is laid out. When the night comes, the people of the neighbourhood gather to the dead person's house. Then they go to the room where the dead person is laid out, and they say their prayers. A member of the family stands at the door of the kitchen, and another at the door of the room where the dead person is laid out to welcome the people. Some one of the neighbours cuts the tobacco and gives a pipe full of it to each man. Long ago the men used to keep the pipes and bring them home. After the men have a smoke, now they hand back the pipes to the owner and are kept. At twelve o'clock the Rosary is recited after which an ologón is started. Tea is then made. Two or three girls of the neighbourhood lay the tables. If a friend comes along distance, he is given a drop of Whiskey and also those who remain in the morning.

The second night the corpse is put to the church. When it is taken outside the door it is left down on two chairs. The chairs on which the coffin is rested outside the door are turned upside-down and left outside that night. The coffin is brought into the house by the people of the same surname. The head of the coffin is brought in first. Before the corpse is put into the coffin, they all start to ologón. Then the coffin is put upon two chairs outside the door, and they all start to ologón again Then the hearse comes, and two or three boys shoulder the coffin as far as it. Long ago it used be brought in the common car and sometimes in a side-car.

Some women of the neighbourhood used sit on the coffin and ologón. If the person is the first member of the family to die, the father and mother go before the hearse. Then on the third day after the death takes place the person is buried. All the people around the place go to the church. About twelve o'clock the funeral leaves the church. Every door is shut while it is passing. When it reaches the graveyard, the grave is dug by two or three boys. Then the coffin is put into the hole. When they start to cover it with the earth, they all start to ologón again. Then the priest recites the prayers at the graveside, and he blesses it. The people of the house bring a pint of holy water and that is left on the grave.

In this parish the coffin is put into the grave with the screws unloosened. The teacher told us a story about a girl from Kerry who was married to a boy from Castletown. She died very soon after her marriage and she was buried in the Castletown graveyard. Her mother who lived in Kerry was at the funeral, and she loosened the screws of the coffin when it was put into the grave, and the people of the place did not know at the time that it was the custom of Kerry.

When the coffin is put into the grave the relatives begin to ologón. The first Saturday night after the person is buried some garment which he wore during his life is put out and the name of the dead person is called three times.

KILMACKOWEN
Natural World and Weather Lore

Wild Animals

There are several wild animals in this place now, but they were more plentiful long ago. Some of them do great harm, while others are very useful. Sometimes young ones are caught and tamed, especially small animals like rabbits. Hares and rabbits are very common wild animals in this parish, and they are also plentiful. Some farmers say that they are great harm, because they eat all their ryegrass and turnips and cabbages. People who have hounds and dogs say that they are very useful, because they provide great pastime for them. When they are caught, they are killed and eaten.

The rabbits make holes down through the ground or through the fence, and it is in these places they live. The hares live up on the hills in what is called a form or a seat. Some of them are very fast runners, and on this account the hunters find it very hard to catch them.

Foxes are very common wild animals in this place, but they are getting scarce of late because everybody kills them. They do great harm sometimes, moreover in the early months of the year. When the lambs are young, they kill them and eat them. They eat hens and ducks, and hares wherever they get them. The fox is not a very useful animal. Some people say that his tongue is very good for taking out thorns. If a fox is caught without harming its skin is sold and people get money for it. Foxes are said to be most clever animals in this part of Ireland, and there are several stories told about them.

The badger is another one of the wild animals. Its colour is usually grey, but sometimes its black. It lives in a hole in the ground, or in the fence. He is very fierce especially when he is caught in his den. They fight very much with dogs and sometimes they kill them. They eat grass and hares, and other kinds of meat, and the roots of trees.

Another animal which is very wild is the otter. He lives near the rivers, and sometimes it is very hard to catch him. He eats fish, so that he is not very harmful. He is useful because his skin can be sold, and it is dear if it is not damaged.

Here is a story of a badger fight. One day my father and Dan Houlihan of Inches went to the hill for sheep. They had two terriers and one sheepdog with them. They were sitting on a little hill, and they saw a badger about twelve yards from them. When the badger saw the men coming towards him, he ran to his den, and tried to smother himself inside. He came out of the den after an hour's watching. He ran towards the terriers and scratched their faces with his front paws. The dogs were covered with blood and could not see their enemy. The badger ran about a hundred yards and my father killed him with his stick. He skinned him and nailed the skin to the back of the door. When it was dry, he took it off and made a carpet of it.

Collector: Dick Donovan, Crumpane, Co. Cork
Informant: Richard Donovan

KILMACKOWEN
History and Archaeology

A Bronze Axe

On a certain day some years ago. The late Paddy Shanahan and his two sons were making drains in a field underneath the village of Goulane, beside the river. They happened to meet with a bronze hatchet. Not knowing what it was, one of them placed it on a stone, while the other was trying to strike it with a sledge. The father, fearing an accident, snatched it from them and flung it into a neighbour's field. Next year as the neighbour was tilling the field, he found the hatched and brought it to Richard Sullivan, Castletown Bere, who sent it away to Dublin, where it can be seen by the public.

A Stone Hammer

In days gone by in one of my fields at Carrig, about a mile north of Kilmacowen school, below the house, was a circle of large standing stones. As they were an obstruction in ploughing. My father, Jeremiah Sullivan and my grandfather rooted them up. In the middle of the circle was a large, round flat slab, supported by boulders. That also they rooted up. They were unable to take up one, and they used powder which refused to go off. Some days later as my father was passing the stone it suddenly went off, and some splinters flew in his face, and he was blind for some time. On the other side of the fence were some standing stones. A few years ago, a certain contractor rooted them up, and beneath one was a stone hammer. One stone yet remains stretched on the ground about 18 feet long.

Collector: Peg Sullivan, Carrig, Co. Cork
Informant: Jerry Sullivan, aged 50

A Hidden Treasure

About a mile from Kilmackowen school there is a great big field. In the middle of this field there is a very large stone - it is about eighteen feet high. It stands in the middle of the field. The old people say that there was a chieftain buried under this stone and that there was money buried with him. This place is very lonesome. The name of this field is Galan. There was another stone standing in the same field. Some years ago, my father and some others knocked it down. They found the bones of a person. This stone was about twenty feet high.

Collector: Ted Harrington, Kilmackowen, Co. Cork
Informant: Jerry Harrington, aged 50

ARDGROOM

Co. Chorcaighe
Bar: Béara
Par: Cill Choitairainn
Scoil: Ardgroom
Oide: R Ó Hurdail

Adrgroom
Local Folklore and Stories

Maire Ni Murcadha

There lived in Drianagh, Eyeries, Castletownbere, a woman named Maire Ni Murcadha. She lived there about the eighteenth century and in the first decades of the nineteenth century. The people did not know much about her until she was about fifty years of age, and it was then she started to set charms. The people were very much afraid of her and did everything she told them because they believed she had some power from the devil. The priests told the people not to do or believe what she told them, but everything that she told was true and the priests finally believed her. There are many stories connected with her and I heard some of them from my grandmother.

There lived in the townland of Pulleen a poor fisherman on whom the people christened the Durdie for a nickname. He was married a few years and his wife got sick. The old people at that time believed very much in fairies and they said that this man's wife was taken by the fairies. The man went to Máire Ní Murcadha and told her how his wife was taken by the fairies. She told him that his wife was in the fairy's castle which was across the harbour from his house. She told him to get a six-oar boat, the strongest oarsmen that he could get, and to go to the fairy's castle the next night and that she would go with them and bring back his wife. The man got the boat and the men and Máire came the next night to go with them. They went into the boat twelve o'clock that night and Máire put them thus: one man on each oar, one on the stern steering the boat, and herself and the Durdie on the stern. They landed in Kerry. Two men stayed in the boat and the remainder went to search for the fairy's castle. They reached the castle three o'clock in the morning and found the woman alone there. They brought her to the boat, and everyone got into his former place. Máire told them to pull as hard as they could until they get to a place in the tide called Thar a Leath Taoidhe because if the fairies would catch them between the land and that place, they would drown them. They got to this place and brought her home. She died shortly after they brought her.

My Grandmother told me a few nights ago that her mother was taken by the fairies and there was an old witch put in the bed instead of her. After some time, they were getting tired and afraid of her, and her father went to Máire Ní Murcadha and told her about she being taken by the fairies. Máire told him that a number of horses would pass by his house the next evening and that his wife will be on the last white horse and to grab her and take her with him. He stood by the end of the house the next evening until the horses came along. His wife was on the last white horse, and he tried to grab her, but the life fell from his hands and legs, and he had to go home without her.

There lived in Claondoire a big strong man named Daniel Riley. He went to the wood one day to cut some spars. When he had about half the spars cut, he got a sudden pain on his knee. The pain was so terrible that he fell almost lifeless to the ground. After an hour or so he got up and went home. He was as good as ever he was for a few months, but the pain came on his knee again and he was almost dead with it. His wife went to Castletown one day for the doctor. On her way she met Máire Ní Murcadha and Máire asked her how her husband was. She told her that he was not well and that she was going to Castletown for the Doctor. Máire told her that she would give her a cure for it because it was a fairy pain. They went to the graveyard in Kilkatherine and Máire took a fist of earth from the man's mother's grave and gave it to the woman. She told her to bring the fist of earth home and rub it to the man's knee. The woman did as she told her and after a few days her husband was cured.

There once lived in Eyeries a woman who was supposed to be in the fairies or to have some supernatural power. Her name was Maire Ní Murcúdha. It seems that all people believed in her. However, the priest at the time whose name was Father Larkin heard about her and he published it from the altar. He gave strict warning to the people not to believe in her and that she was possessed by the devil. One night he had to come to Ardgroom on a sick call. At that time there were no motors or bicycles. It was on horseback they usually travelled. The priest came on horseback this night and with him came another man on his own horse. When they were returning home, they met a headless coach followed by a band of fairies. When the priest was passing them, he was pulled off his horse and he received a few hard blows. When he came to himself, he went on his horse and rode away. After a while he was called back and given his hat which he lost during the fight. He continued his journey and tried to overtake his comrade, but he did not. He went to bed that night and pretended his adventure to nobody. A few days later he met Maire Ní Murcúdha and she asked him why did he published from the altar about herself. She told him not to do it again or if he would that he would get more strokes than what he got that night. "It was I gave you your hat and only for me you would not be here today." From that day off, the priest never spoke a word about Maire, nor was he ever bothered by her.

Collector: Brid Ní Ceilleacair, Bunskellig, Co. Cork
Informant: Timothy Kelleher

There lived in Glenbeg a young girl. One night she stayed up minding a sick cow. She got turf to put on the fire. When she was putting it on the fire one of the sods was thrown at her by a fairy and it struck her on the leg, and it got very sore. The next morning one of her neighbours was on the mountain about six o clock to see his cattle. He met a woman and he said to her, "Is not it early you are out?" and she answered, "I was in Glenbeg last night. I did not like to be there at all because there is a poor girl there and I am afraid she will have a sore leg as she got a stroke from a fairy last night. I would not like to do anything to her father, but I had to do it." That woman was Maire Ní Murcadha who lived in Eyeries who was supposed to be in the fairies.

Collector: Anna Kelleher, Bunskellig, Co. Cork
Informant: Timothy Kelleher

Long ago the old people used to say that an old fairy woman used to be seen by Bawers every night at nightfall. One night there was a man named John Sheehan from Ardgroom going to Adrigole to his cousin's wake. When he was returning home, he saw an old fairy woman by Bawers bridge. He had a pocketknife in his pocket, and he held it in his hand. She never touched him. When he was passing Ardgroom school he met a man going west the road. He told him that there was an old fairy woman west by Bawers bridge and to be very careful of her. The man kept going west and when he was passing Bawers bridge the woman came out in the road and she hit him on the knee. His knee was very sore from that on.

One night his mother was talking to Máire Ní Murcada. Máire told her to go to the grave-yard and bring clay from it, that it cured a man before. On the following night the mother went to the graveyard at 12 o'clock and brought some of the clay. The man's leg cured but it was always a bit short.

Collector: Una Ní Neill, Ardgroom, Co. Cork
Informant: Jeremiah O Neill, parent

Long ago there lived in Glenuinsquin a man. He was married a few years. They had one child about seven months old. One night his wife fell sick. She was sick for many months, and she was unable to eat any food. So, he heard he would get a cure for her. One day as he was on a visit to Eyeries he met Maire Ní Murcada, and she asked him how was his wife? "She is no good these few months. Muise mo grian í [she is my sunshine]." "You poor fool, for your wife is far from being good." "What are you saying?" says he. "Oh! For your wife is long with the fairies. That old granóg you have is not your own at all." He asked her advice, and she told him to go to Adrigole to a place called Líos Mór. She told him that two men riding on horseback would be leading the fairy's army, and that his wife would be on the second horse. "Bring seven men with you and cross the hill and ye will meet me on the top of the hill." So, he promised and on the night appointed he left the house. He brought seven men and himself. When they went up to the hill, they met Máire Ní Murcada. They travelled southwards until they arrived at Liós Mór. They sat at the entrance of the Líos until the fairy's army arrived. Sitting on the second horse they saw his wife. Máire made a grab for her and brought her safe. At the minute Maire grabbed her, all the fairies disappeared. They travelled home with her. Máire Ní Murcada went in and reddened a shovel in the fire and told the old fairy woman to sit on it. As soon as she told her, the fairy went to run, and Máire hit her with the shovel on the head. She disappeared and was never heard of again.

Collector: Peig Ní Seaghdha, Ardgroom, Co. Cork
Informant: Mrs Healy, grandmother

How Béara got its Name

This promontory is called the Béara peninsula. On one side of Béara lies Bantry Bay, and on the other side, Kenmare Bay. There are a lot of old stories of how Béara got its name. This is one I heard at home, and we do not know if it is true or not.

There were two Kings in Ireland long ago. Their names were Eógan Mór and Con Cead Cátha. Both wanted to become High King of Ireland. They were fighting about it. After some time Eógan Mór went to Spain to help fight against Con Cead Cátha. Then they fought and after a while Ireland was divided between them. Con Cead Cátha got the north half of Ireland and Eógan Mór got the other side. The north side was called Leat-Cuinn and the other side was called Leat-Bhó. During Eogáin's visit to Spain he got married to a daughter of the King of Spain. The name of the girl was Béara. They came to Cill Mhic Eogain to live and that is the reason why this place was called Béara.

Collector: Ann Hartnett, Ardgroom, Co. Cork
Informant: Patrick Hartnett

The Woman who Stole the Butter

In the year 1864 there lived on a hill in Kerry a woman who had one cow. She used to come down the hill into Sneem every market day. That woman with one cow used to have a large crock full of butter. She used to come once a week. One day while she was in the market, she fell in a weakness, and they put her to the hospital. They thought she would die. So, they sent for the priest. When the priest came, she got a little better and she was able to make a confession. She said out loud to all that were listening that she had a woman's butter which she got by a charm. She also said she was sorry. She recovered from her illness and went home. The Tuesday after was market day and she was coming to the market. She had a great crock of butter which would weigh about forty pounds. She met an angel who was sitting on a rock and the angel asked her whose butter had she. She said it was her own. The angel said, "What is yours shall be yours." She hit the crock with a stick and only one pound remained in its form. The rock is now called Carraig an Ime. The old woman was never seen at the market again.

Collector: Úna Ní Néill, Ardgroom, Co. Cork
Informant: Jeremiah O' Neill, father

Glenmore – Pot of Gold

There lived a man in Glenmore, and he had one of the high boots full of gold. He was taken sick and was telling the old woman day by day that he would tell her before he'd die where the gold was, and by night he went out and hid it. If she might watch him, she might have a chance. The day he died then when he was in a dying way, she asked him where was the gold hidden. He said in a triopall of rushes and that it was no good for her that the ground grew over it, and that it was no good for her when she didn't watch him hiding it.

Collector: Peig Ní Seagdha, Ardgroom, Co. Cork
Informant: Mrs Healy

Coís – Pot of Gold

There was a man long ago and he dreamt that a pot of gold was buried in Coís. One morning he rose and got two men, and they went to Coís. They dug down but they didn't get the gold. They came in again and the same man dreamt that he was very near to it, but that he would have to bring another man with him. The second night they went out and they brought another man with them. The dug down until they came to a slat, but it was too late in the night to take up the stone. They came home again that night and the same man dreamt that the gold was under the slat, but that one of the men would have to lose their life. When he rose in the morning he told the men about his dream, so they didn't go out anymore.

The Rock at Faill a Cluigig

There are many old stories by the people around this place. Some of them are about castles and more of them are about seines in the strand. My father told me one the other night. This one is about noise heard in a rock. There is a place in Pulleen called Faill a Cluigig. It is a big cliff about a hundred feet high. At the bottom of the cliff there is a rock, and it is supposed to be haunted. Long ago the people used to draw shells up from the sea to this cliff. One day when they were coming up to the cliff, they heard the noise in the rock. They heard it again and again. It was a woman making a churn. She was singing and rocking a cradle. Then they heard the child crying. After a while they heard a pig grunting, and then the rock started to move away. Sometime after a woman went up to the cliff to catch seagulls. She was going up the cliff and she heard the crying. A man followed her, and he caught her. He brought her into a lovely palace. After a while he took her out and they went over to the Kerry side. After a year or so the woman came home and lived in peace until she died.

Collector: Ann Hartnett, Ardgroom, Co. Cork
Informant: Patrick Hartnett

The Clever Wife

There once lived a man named the Gúbán Saór. He very clever but he had a son who was not. He wanted a clever girl to marry his son. One day he gave a sheepskin to his son. He told him sell it and bring back the money and the skin. The son told him that he could not do so, so he went to the fair. He was in the fair all day, but he could not sell it. When he was coming home, he met a girl and he told her his story. The girl told him to come to the house. The girl got a sheers, shore the wool off the skin, and gave the boy the money for the wool. When they went home, he told his father all that had happened. The Gúbán said that he would make a match between the girl and his son. He made the match and they married.

The Gúbán Saor was a great mason and a king sent for him to build a house. When they were going the boy's wife told them to be very nice to the girls of the house. When they were going along the Gúbán told his son to shorten the road. The boy said that he didn't know how so the Gúbán sent him home. He told his wife and she told him to tell stories. He caught up to his father again and he began telling stories. They reached the place and they started to build a house. When they had the house nearly finished, they told the Gúbán that the king was going to kill them. The Gúbán told the King that he could not finish the house without one thing and that he would send his son home for it. The King would not leave his son go, sending one of his men. The Gúbán put down on the paper, 'Crooked against Crooked,' and 'Straight against Straight.' When the boy's wife saw this she knew what was wrong and she told the King's man to stoop into a big chest and that he would get the instrument there. He fell into the chest, and she locked him inside in it. She wrote to the King, and she said that she would not leave the man back until her husband and his father would come home. So, they were released.

Collector: Una Ní Neill, Ardgroom, Co. Cork
Informant: Jeremiah O'Neill

Tuirin a Bullaig

Long ago the people had many old plans, and old cures which are not to be seen or heard of nowadays. There is a great big rock up at the top of the hill at a place called Tuirin a bullaig. The rock is made the shape of an altar. There was a head man of the Danes, and he ordered all his men to be at this rock for a certain time in the day. Then the head man used to read to them from a big book and they answer him in return. This mass was called Aifreainn na madraí. They continued this for some time. The parish priest ordered them to leave the place and not to be mocking mass. So, they left, and they were distributed around from place to place. Then they made a líos and went to live in it, and those places are to be seen still. The parish priest came to the altar a few weeks ago and he said it was no altar, but it was some kind of an old resting place they had.

Collector: Una Ní Neill, Ardgroom, Co. Cork
Informant: Jeremiah O Neill

The Story of Two Giants

Long ago there lived two giants whose names were Glug and Grug. They were very fond of each other. The king did not want them to live in his palace because they used to steal all the fowl from their neighbours. One of them was a very small man and the other was very tall, because every time he passed by, the people used think they had night.

One day the king made up his mind to gather all his fighting men and that he would give them any request they would ask if they killed the giants. So, they went to the giants' house and when they reached the place the giants were asleep. The king called them, and they came out, so both parties fought together. The king and his men were no match for the giants, so they had to return home.

There was an old woman living at the foot of a hill and she had one son named Sean. Her husband was dead. Sean had two friends a mouse and a bee. When Seán heard of the giants, he went to the king and brought with him his two comrades. He told the king he would kill the giants if he gave him anything he would ask for. When the neighbours saw Seán going to kill the giants with a mouse and a bee to fight with him, they laughed loudly. Seán walked on and paid no attention to them, until he reached the giants' house. At first the mouse nibbled a hole in the door. Then Seán put it in his hand and opened the door. So, the three comrades stepped inside and went into the bedroom. The two giants were fast asleep. The mouse began to eat one of the giants' ears and the bee stung his nose. "Stop Glug!" roared brother grog, "or I will roll your head off around the floor." The bee kept on stinging and the mouse kept on biting. The two brothers jumped out on the floor. One of them got an axe and he hit his brother on the head and his head rolled around the floor. Then the two brothers died, and the three comrades went back to the king enjoying the great deed they had done. "What will ye be asking?" said the king. "A thimble full of honey every day as long as I live said the bee." "You can have it in welcome." "As much corn as will feed me while I will live," said the mouse. "With all my heart said the king." "As much money as will build a house and buy a farm and live a rich life." "With all my heart." said the king. The three friends got their requests and lived a good life afterwards.

The Story of a Fairy Cow

There was once a farmer, and he had a sick cow. So, one of the neighbours told him to kill the cow and he did. One day when he was skinning the cow a beggar woman called the way and asked him for alms. So, he cut off the cow's head and gave it to her. She thanked him and walked along. She came to the next house, and she asked for permission to boil the meat. The woman put the meat in water, and it boiled the following day. The man and his wife went to mass, and they left the children and the old woman minding the house. When the meat was boiled the children asked the old woman for some of it. The woman went to the pot, and she took off the cover off the pot and what was inside but the head of a Christian. The children got such a fright that they never stopped running until they reached the church. Then the priest came to the house, and he ordered the head to be buried. He also sent word to the owner of the cow and told him to bury the cow because she was a fairy cow.

Collector: Úna Ní Néill, Ardgroom, Co. Cork
Informant: Jeremiah O Neill, father

The Unfortunate Mother

About seventy years ago there lived a woman in Glenbeg. She had eighteen children. When the eighteenth child was born, which was a girl, the father took her to the church to be baptised. One of the older girls stayed at home minding her mother. The woman told the girl to get all her new clothes. Then the woman put on her clothes. After this she told the girl to go down in the room and that she would get another baby under the bed. The girl did as she was told and saw an old witch in the bed. While the girl was in the room the woman went out and went up the hill. When the people came home from the church the girl told her story. The woman in bed was very sick, so the man of the house sent for the priest and doctor. The priest anointed the old woman. Then the man told the story to the priest, and the priest said he could do nothing now.

Collector: Aine Ní Cheilleachair, Bunskellig, Co. Cork
Informant: Timothy Kelleher

The Stolen Daughter

There was once a farmer who lived in Kerry. He had an only daughter. He also had a big farm and there was a líos in it. He kept a pig. It was Christmas time and the farmer, his wife and daughter went to the town for the Christmas messages. As they were passing a public house the farmer and his wife went in for a drink and the girl stayed outside. She told them not to be long. When they came out, she was angry with them for being so long. They went home together and when the daughter got up next day, she was unable to walk. From that day until the fifteenth day of April the girl was very bad. She was unable to eat anything. The doctor and nurse attended to her every week. They had her given up for death. The farmer got a servant boy for sticking the sgiollans and they ran short of sgiollans so they sent the servant boy home for some. As he was passing the window, he saw an old fairy woman inside and she eating potatoes. She had big, long teeth. The boy got such a fright that he brought no sgiollans and he never stopped running until he reached the field. He told the farmer his story. "Sha," said the farmer, "My daughter is gone and that one is given in place of her." The farmer ran home as fast as he could, and he never stopped running until he reached one of his neighbours. Two young boys came into the farmer's house. They made a big fire and they reddened a shovel in it. They ran to the bedroom and they told the girl sit into the shovel. She made a jump and out the door. The two men followed her, and she ran into the líos. They heard all the noise inside and with that out jumped the farmer's daughter. They brought her home. She is married now and has a large family.

Collector: Una Ní Néill, Ardgroom, Co. Cork
Informant: Jeremiah O Neill

The Cailleach Béara

There once lived in Dursey an old witch whose name was the Cailleach Béara. One morning she made up her mind to pay a visit to her sister who lived in Ardfert, and by night she went there unknown. While she was with her sister, she heard that the priest was talking about her, and she made up her mind to come back. She took one step from Ardfert to Pullen, and from Pullen to Cumindach, and another step from Cumindach to Dursey. The sign of her foot is to be seen plainly on the tops of those mountains still. When she came back, she started fighting about what he was saying. The priest said to her that he would never again talk about her, and he got so frightened that he never spoke about her again. She was all right until another new priest came to the parish. She started fighting to him too, and tried to frighten him, but the priest was too clever for her. One day she was fighting him, and he ran after her. He caught her by Kilcatherine school and turned her into a rock. She also had a bucket on her arm. She is to be seen always turned into a rock, and the shape of the bucket on her arm.

Collector: Peig Ní Sheaghdha, Ardgroom, Co. Cork
Informant: Mrs Mary Healy

The Hare that Stole the Milk

Once there lived in Lauragh a woman and she had the devil's power. She was bad friends with her neighbours. Every morning when they used to go out to milk the cows, they would have but one cup of milk between four of them. One morning, one of the men got up early and went out to watch what was making the cows so dry. He was a good while there when he saw coming towards him, a small hare. The man had a hound with him, but he said to himself that he would not set the hound after the hare for a while until he would see where the hare would go. After a while the hare walked away into the cabin and got the stool. After a while she started milking the cows, and the man, thinking she was real, put the hound after her. The hound followed her but could not catch her until he came to a stone wall off an old house, and he caught her jumping over the wall. He caught her by the back and killed her. That evening he went into the old house to see the hare. What would he see, but a puddle of blood, and a woman dead by the side of the blood? He screamed and ran home, and by the time he reached home his wife was dead. He afterwards said that it was better to leave the milk of the four cows with the old witch than his wife.

Collector: Peggie Shea, Ardgroom, Co. Cork
Informant: Michael Sheehan

The Strange Seaweed Cutters

There lived a man and his wife in a very backward place near the seashore. They were married a good number of years. They had one daughter and when she reached the age of twenty years, she emigrated to America. Day by day her parents were getting old and feeble and drawing nearer to the grave. At last, they wrote to her and told her to make up her mind to come home. So, she did. She remained with her parents for one year. Then she got married and her father got into bad health. One morning he got up at daybreak and went out to look around and opposite him was a long rock called Carraig na Seagaí. He saw a boat and three men, and they were cutting seaweed. He kept on watching in amazement, saying to himself who would be cutting seaweed at that hour. He looked again and they were still there, but they disappeared under water. He went in and told his wife his story. He ate not breakfast and went to bed. His wife went to the cabin to milk the cows and when she returned, he was dead in bed.

Never look back

There once lived in Canfaí a man and a woman. They used be up every night until about four o'clock in the morning. Long ago the people used believe very much in fairies out by night and other queer objects. The way of living this man had was fishing. He used to go out every night during the fishing season. Some nights he might get a lot of fish and others he would not get any one at all. Every night that he would have about four or five hundred fish he used to go to Kenmare. His wife used to go with him some of the nights and they use to leave another old woman after them at home. This old woman was very sick this night, and she asked the woman to stay with her, but she refused and went with her husband. When they were about two miles out from Kenmare, they met this enormous white hound, and he was the full breath of the road.

They passed by in safety, but the woman being so curious looked back and saw a big crowd of people standing on the same place where the hound was standing. The man was very vexed to the woman, for he said it was not right to look back when you are going on a journey by night. Nothing happened them until they reached Kenmare when they were not able to sell any bite of their fish in the market. It was then their bad luck began. They had to return home without selling the fish. They were about the same place where they met the hound when they felt the heavy load on the back of the car. The man looked back this time and he saw the old woman sitting on the shaft of the car. She stayed there until they came to a lane about a mile from their own house turning down to the sea. When they came home the old woman they left at home was dead, and she was changed. The man said I suppose it was she that was after them from Kenmare. It was she that was there all right said the woman, and that she must be in the crowd of women that they saw near Kenmare. The man said she will haunt us through life and that it was no wonder we did not sell the fish in Kenmare.

Collector: Peggie Shea, Ardgroom, Co. Cork
Informant: Mrs Healy

The Púca

About twenty years ago the people did a lot of fishing around here. Every dark night they used to go out with a seine to catch mackerel. There were about sixteen men joined on the seine altogether. They used leave a strand called Cuas and go as far as a place called Dúna to see would they see any fish. Every night when the men used come to the strand, they used sit down on a rock by the strand until it used to get dark. As soon as it used get dark an object like a horse used run out of the water and gallop up the strand. He used do the same thing every night. When they used come in he used be running around a field near the strand pulling chains after him. At length the men got afraid of him, and they used to go out before it used get dark.

One night when they came to the strand it began to rain. They went under the tarpaulin which they had for covering the seine when they had it inside. The púca came out and jumped over the men without touching them. They did not see him for about a month after that, and they thought he was gone.

One night they caught a lot of fish. When one man went home, he sent his two sons to the strand for fish he left under the tarpaulin. The púca hunted them and they went under the tarpaulin and stayed there for the night until the morning. They called him the púca for that reason. He went away in the end himself.

Collector: Timothy Sullivan

Stealing Butter

I heard a story being told by an old man about taking butter. There were people in Kerry whose calves died for five years. They used try every plan to keep the calves alive but it was a failure. They could make no butter or could not drink the milk after putting it into the churn. It was like that for five years, and one night they heard a cow bellowing in the cabin. The man went out, and he left a boy and a girl in the house after him. He closed the door on them, and while he was out the door opened. They shut the door, and after a while it opened again. A woman stood in the door, and put in her head but did say not any word. "Get the holy water," said the girl to the little boy. He got the holy water and threw it on her. She disappeared at once and was never seen again. The woman went to Kenmare a few days after. She met a woman who was a great friend of hers, and the woman told her that she had this woman's butter for five years. From that day off the calves lived, and they were able to make their churns. It was said that the other woman had taken the butter by a charm she had set.

Collector: Peggie Shea, Ardgroom, Co. Cork
Informant: Mrs Healy

ADRGROOM
People, Places and Property

Wardin

Long ago there lived a man named Wardin. He was a landlord. Himself and the priest were always disagreeing. He was very strict with his tenants. He evicted a very poor man off his land on account of not paying his rent. He would not allow him build a little house in any part of his property. The parish priest gave him permission to build a little bungalow in the churchyard. Wardin wanted to evict him, but the priest would not allow him do so. Wardin wanted him to pay rent. The priest told the landlord that he had no claim to the churchyard, so both of them were disputing about it. The priest preached from the alter that he would make an example of him before the people. Soon after, Wardin got sick, and he was made deaf and dumb. and crippled He was sent to Dublin, and he was not cured there. He came home again. He died at home, and he was buried in the protestant church yard. It is said the no grass ever grew on his grave. The clay is as fresh as the day he was buried there.

Collector: Eileen Ní Neill, Ardgroom, Co. Cork
Informant: Jeremiah O Neill

Murty Óg Ó Súilleabháin

Murty Óg was born at Cualagh in the eighteenth centaury. When he was very young his parents died. A woman on Dursey Island took him to her house and reared him. When he was about eighteen years, he left Dursey and went to Spain where he joined the Irish Brigade. After some time, he came back to Ireland. He started smuggling. He used to bring wool and men to Spain, and he used to bring back wine and tobacco. Once while he was at home, he met Puxley on his way to Castletown and Puxley was against smuggling. Murty shot him. Then he had to run from the English. He still carried on smuggling. He had a house in Eyeries beag and a servant named Donal Ó Conaill. Once he came home from Spain and he stayed in the house for a few days. The English heard that he was there and came there across the hill from Dunboy. A friend of Murty was with the English and he fired a shot when he came near the house. The English shot him for doing this. They came to the house, and they put the roof of the house in fire as it was a thatch one. Murty ran out and as he was crossing the river he was shot. They tied his head on to a boat and pulled him after it to Cork. His head was cut off and put on a spike on the gate of the prison as it was a custom at that time.

Mo Cheantar Féin

The townland I live in is called Bunskellig. This townland got its name as it is at the bottom of Skeilg hill. There are seven houses in it now, but long ago it contained of fifteen houses. There is a beautiful lake in Glenbeg. The parish I live in is called Eyeries, but long ago it was called the parish of Cill Ciathiarn. In the cemetery in the point of Cill Ciathiarn stands the ruins of an old church. The old people said that this church was built in the year one thousand about the time of Brian Boru. This peninsula is called the Barony of Béara. We have an old story which tells us how Béara got its name. There were two Kings in Ireland about the time of St Patrick, Eogán mór and Con Ceadh Cata. A battle was fought between them as they both wanted to become High King. Eogán went to Spain looking for help. While he was away, he married the daughter of the King of Spain, whose name was Béara. He landed in a place called Claondra and to honour his wife he called this peninsula, Béara. There is a place in Béara called Cill Mic Eogáin, meaning The Burial place of the son of Eogan.

Collector: Anna Kelleher, Bunskellig, Co. Cork
Informant: Timothy Kelleher

Names of Rocks

There are a lot of old rocks which have very peculiar names. These are some of them. Carraig na Seagaí: When it is low water all the seagais gather and go on this rock, and that is why it is called Carraig na Seagaí. Cloch Tarbh: Because it is made the same shape as a bull. Cloc na Socraide: Long ago when the corpse used be carried to the church born on the shoulders of the pall bearers, when they used to come to the top of hill they used to take a rest on top of this rock. Carraig an Figirne: Every Sunday and holidays all the young crowd used to gather to this rock, and anybody would not be allowed to come but somebody that would tell the truth. Cloc na Fiallán: At the middle of a lake there is a big round rock and all the seagulls perch on it. Máire Caoc: There was an old woman living there long ago and she lived in a little thatched cottage and at the entrance at the door was a big rock where she used always sit and talk to herself.

ADRGROOM
Farming, Trade and Crafts

Flainín

Most of the clothes which we wear now are manufactured, but up until about twenty years ago the people used to make their own flannel which was far warmer than the clothes we wear now. They used sheer the sheep first, and wash the wool. After that they used comb it, that is to free it out of each other, and make little rolls of it. Then they used put it to the mill to be carded, that is to make rolls of it with enough wool in each roll to make a thread. It was brought home then and spun into bulicins, and a ball was made out of the bulicins. It used be spun the second time to double the thread of the bulicin. It used be put to the weaver then and he used to make flannel for the people who used not make flannel themselves.

There is still a woollen mill in the village of Ardgroom. It is the mill which cards all the wool for Ardgroom and is worked by water. It used be warped to take the twists out of it. Two sticks would be put into the wall, and the thread would be put under one stick and over the other. It would be put on like that until six hundred threads would be on the sticks. It used be brought to the weaver after that, and he would make flannel of it. It used be scoured then to make it warm. and fine. After that it used be worn.

Collector: Timothy Sullivan, Ardgroom, Co. Cork
Informant: Flur Sullivan

Turning

All the farmers are preparing the ground for the gardens now as the weather is very fine. We usually plough our garden as the fields are fairly big. Some farmers turn the ground as the fields are small and rough. When turning, it is necessary for two people to be standing near each other. The man on the outside cuts the sods with two attempts. The man in the inside puts his spade under the sod and they turn it to the left. The man on the outside has harder work because he must lift the sod. At first, they turn one side of the ridge, then they go to the other side and turn another sod up against that one. They leave what is called a bone between the two ridges. They turn this afterwards. They split it in the middle and turn half of it to each ridge. When this is done, they break the sods and form a bed for the potatoes. Then the potatoes are cut into sgiollans, usually by the woman of the house or by a crowd of women. When they are cutting the sgiollans it is necessary for them to leave eyes in the sgiollans so as they will grow. If they do not set the sgiollans for a week or so they put lime on them. It is usually the young girls that stick the sgiollans and then they close the holes in the evening before stopping work, for fear that the night would rain and the sgiollans would get destroyed.

Collector: Anna Kelleher, Bunskellig, Co. Cork
Informant: Timothy Kelleher

ADRGROOM
Local Customs

Piseoga

The old people believe in piseogs as they used long ago. They say it is not right if you were making a churn to have your neighbour go out without striking a turn. They say he would bring the butter with him. They say it is not right to throw feet water in the night. They say it is not right if you had a house above the road to build a new house below the road. They say it is not right to remove the fireplace of a house. They say it is not good to sleep alone in a new house without getting somebody of the same name with you. It is not right to enter a new house the first time without bringing something with you. They also say it is not right to sit on the path. There is a story connected with it. It is not right to walk over a person when he is sitting down because he would not grow any more. A whistling woman and a crowing hen there is never no luck in the house they are in. If men are going fishing and if they meet a red-haired woman, they won't catch any fish. They also say if a frog comes in the house at night-time it is the sign of death.

If a wedding met a funeral the people who got married will have no luck. It is not right to carry anything on your shoulder when entering a house. It is not right to bring milk to another house on May Day. It is not right to bring milk to another house and to bring it back in again. When a woman is getting married it is an old saying that she should wear something old, something new, something borrowed, and something blue.

The old people believe it is not right to do this or not to do that. They think it would break the law if you would not believe in them. The following are some of their piseogas. It is not right to burn white thorns in the fire as the fairies would come into the house. It is not right to bring out a coal of fire while you are making a churn. It is not right to leave the water which you had washing your feet inside at night. A person living above the road should not go to live in a new house below the road. It is not right to build a new house on a path as the fairies would make great noise in the house at night. It is not right to start work on the cross day of the year. It is not right to start work on a Monday. If a calf was sick and if a man would take off his shirt and if he would strike the calf with his shirt, he would get all right. If a calf had a worm and if you made the sign of the cross over him three times and at the same time knotted a cord three times, he would get better. When the old people used be going out by night they thought they would keep away the fairies if they turned their coats inside out, or if they brought burned coals with them. If they brought a lit bit of fir, a black handle knife or a hazel stick, the fairies would disappear as soon as they would see any of these.

Patterns

We had a holiday from school last Friday in this area on account of a pattern which was held where a saint lived about a hundred years ago. There is a pattern there every year on July 8th in honour of Saint Quinnlan. There is a small lake in the middle of a field, and along side the lake there is a big height on which the ruins of the house where the saint lived are still to be seen. This old ruin is now covered with furze except one stone in the middle of the height. Around this height the people make their round. Long ago there were three islands, and every July 8th these islands used to move. Those islands were called triples. In later years a soldier bought the farm in which this field was, and he thought that this lake was destroying the field next to it. So, one morning himself and his son started to drain the field next to the lake, and they also cut a short drain out from the lake. After a while the man said that it was time to stop. He went to bed that night as good as he went any night before that. When he woke in the morning he was crippled and one eye blind. Everybody said then it was not right for him to touch the lake. There is only a little well to be seen there now. Where the rest of the lake was it is all growing with forget-me-nots and other wildflowers. They say a few people got cured out of this well.

This is the way the people make the round. At first when you go into the field you go up to the top of the height and start the rosary. Then you pick up five stones, and do one round around the height, and while you go around you say one decade of the rosary. It is the stone you start to go around, when you come back to the stone again you kneel down and finish your decade and throw one stone. You then start another decade and go around. When you come to the stone again you throw away one stone and finish your decade, and so on until you finish your decades of the rosary. When you finish, you make the sign of the cross on the stone and kiss it. There is usually one or two poor people there, and every person give sixpence or a shilling to each of them.

Then you go down to the well and you say seven Our Fathers, seven Hail Marys, and seven Glory Be to the Fathers, and bless yourself with the water. If you have any sore, you wash it with the water and take three sips of the water. Then you have your round made.

The old people go home after making their rounds, but the young people have some amusement. Most of them go to the dance and stay there all night dancing or drinking porter or whiskey.

Christmas Customs

We are back to school again today after our Christmas holiday. We all enjoyed Christmas well. It is over now. The evening before Christmas I went to confession in Ardgroom church. I received Holy Communion on Christmas day. The old people kept up the old customs such as, anyone should not light the Christmas candles except the youngest in the house. All the people decorate their houses inside with holly, and with tinsel. Some people keep drink in their houses for Christmas night such as whiskey and stout for the old people. The priest usually says two Masses on Christmas day. One at half nine and the other at half ten. Most people go to first Mass and are home in time to cook the dinner. They usually have chicken on Christmas day. All the young people go to the dance Christmas day night. All the young boys go in the wren St Stephens day. They dress very funny. They wear bags as clothes and carry big wren bushes decorated with holly and wren paper. All the old people go walking New Year's night after supper. Long ago before eating their supper the man of the house used to get up from the table and used take hold of a big cake which was made for that night. He used to go to the door and strike the cake against the door three times. While doing this he used say these words, 'Fograimh an gorta go tir na dTurgach go bhlian o anocht féin go fireanach.' Then they used all gather around it and used eat it.

Collector: Anna Kelleher, Bunskellig, Co. Cork
Informant: Timothy Kelleher

ADRGROOM
Local Cures

Old Cures

There are many old cures around this place. Some of them would cure you, but the others would not. These are some pains that I heard their cure. A herb grows on the ground that would cure toothache. If you washed sore eyes with boracic powder and hot water, they would get better. Carrageen would cure sore throat. If you lent on a sore leg, it would get worse so you should get a crutch to lean on. If you put borax and honey on a sore tongue, it would get better. Iodine would cure cuts.

It was said that Maíre Ní Murcada had a lot of cures for anyone that would be hurt by the fairies, because she used be with them. She cured many persons with her cures.

All the old cures which were there long ago are still carried on nowadays. I often see my mother use these old cures still.

If you got toothache, you should chew the leg of a frog or to get soot and chew it. The old people say that is a great cure for toothache. Instead of using powder for keeping babies skin cool, the old cure they had for it was to get leaves of briars and roast them until they get very hard. Then take them between your hands and rub them very hard until they get as fine as flour. Then shake them on the baby's skin. If you cut your hand or foot, there is a herb that grows on the ground. It is a kind of a leaf and put with the cut it will stop the blood. Carrageen Moss used after cooking is good for a cold. For sore eyes, wash them with tea every morning. To cure a burn, rub ink or put soda with it after burning. Borax and honey are good for a sore tongue. If a dog had the habit of eating eggs, put a red coal of fire into his mouth. For corns, steep ivy leaves in vinegar overnight. If a needle or glass went through your foot, keep rubbing that spot with a black cloth and whatever went in would come out. For a nosebleed, put a cold stone on the back of your head and lay back. For earache, put hot water under your ear. We are not sure if all these cures do good or not some would, and others would not.

The old people had lots of old cures and spells. They believed that many things could be cured by the power of the devil. These are some of their old cures.

When a calf is dying, knot a cord three times over him and at the same time say three times, 'Glory be to the Father.' When a person has some certain disease in his stomach, he will get cured if he will boil dandelion and camomile and drink the water which he used in boiling it. If a person has a wart on his skin, it will go off if he will make the sign of the cross over it three times with your finger after spitting on it for nine mornings before your breakfast. If a person has rheumatism, it will go away if he will carry a potato in his pocket. If you have a boil, it will get better if you will wash it with water which you got in a hole in a rock. If you have a sprained ankle and if you put it under a spout, it will get better.

ADRGROOM
History and Archaeology

A Líos

There are two líoses in the neighbourhood of this townland. One is situated in Droumard and the other in Líos na gCath. We hear many stories in connection with the líos in Droumard. There was a man who lived near the líos. On his way home from Mass one Sunday he went to see the cows that were in a field near the líos. He went the near way to the field, and he had to go over the top of the líos. As he passed by it, he heard a baby crying, and a cradle rocking.

The líos is a circular shape surrounding a deep trench and an earthen wall. It is supposed that it was the Danes who built it. On the top there is a chimney made of stone, with no mortar to keep it together. On one side there is the hole and inside the hole there is a number of steps. Some people went into it this year, and they dug some of the earth, and they found a spear there. There is a hole coming from the líos through two or three fields and coming to an end on the strand which is about three or four hundred yards from it.

Collector: Peig Ní Seagdha, Ardgroom, Co. Cork
Informant: Mrs Healy

LEHID

Co. Ciarraí
Bar: Glenn an Ruachtaigh
Par: Tuaith Ó Siosta
Scoil: Leithead
Oide: Diarmuid Ó Súlleabháin

LEHID
Local Folklore and Stories

Tim Crowley, the Widow's Son

Long ago there lived a widow who was very poor. She had only one son whos was Tim Crowley. He was very fond of night walking and cardplaying. One night as he was coming home, he met a dog. The dog held him up and asked him where he had been all night. He told him where he was cardplaying. The dog told him that he should come with himself now. Crowley asked and begged of him to leave him go home to his old mother who was in delicate health and very sick. The dog granted his request and left him go home, but he had to promise him faithfully that he would meet him again at the same place when the twelve months would be up. He was up to his promise and met the dog at the same place again a year later. He told the dog that his mother was very bad, and she had no other one else to take care of her. He requested him to leave him home to her because she was going to die any minute. The dog left him home again for twelve months more. When next Sunday came Crowley went to mass as usual. He used not go into the Church but stay outside the sacristy door. When mass was going on, a small man came into Crowley and said to him, 'Crowley you are a good man if your courage doesn't fail on you tonight.' He told Crowley to be in such a place that night at twelve o'clock where a hurling match was going to be on between north Kerry and south Kerry with the people of the other world. Crowley did as he was told, and he arrived at a long hall. He sat down inside the door of the hall. He was not long there when six men came in, each one having a hurley. They left their hurleys down sideways in the hall while themselves went into the dining room. The six men never noticed Crowley sitting in the hall. After a little while they came back again for their hurleys and one of the hurleys was missed by the men. Who did they see standing in the hall but Crowley and he having one hurley? They asked him to give them their hurley. He said he would not give it that he was able to use it himself. They told him to come along with and to use it, so he went away with them to the field where they were going to be playing the hurling game. They started the match, and they were not long playing when Crowley put out a goal against north Kerry. The south Kerry players took him up in their shoulders ten times around the field. He gained the field that night. They told him to go home and that he would be alright, that he was safe.

Next Sunday came and he attended mass again as usual, and the same man came to him again at the same place. The man said to him again the second time that he was a good man if his courage didn't fail him that night. He told him to be in such a place again tonight at the same hour as he went before. Crowley went home and waited until the night came and did as he was told. He started away to the same place at the same hour until he came to this long hall as before. He was not long inside when six men came in and they carrying a coffin on their shoulders. They left it down in the hall and went into the dining room. While they were inside in the dining room what did Crowley do but take the coffin away home with him. When the six men returned back the coffin was gone, and they searched all over for it but could not find it. Crowley went again to mass on the third Sunday and this small little man came again. He told him to go the same place as he was before. He was not long inside when a big party came in and went into the dining room. The party that came in were talking about the coffin that was stolen. Where was Crowley but listening to what they were saying. One of them said that it was a pity to leave the young girl go with him that was inside in the coffin. Another one of them said that the girl was no good to Crowley except she would get three drinks of that bottle there in the table. He said to the other one the first drink she would get of the bottle she would breathe, the second drink she would get she would open her eyes, and the third drink she would get she would rise up in her body. Crowley being a hidden inside the door made a dash for the bottle and made off home with it. When Crowley went home, he did as he heard them saying. He gave her three sups of the bottle and as soon as he did, she got quite alright. She looked around her and spoke to Crowley, and told him that it would be no good unless he got the best white horse in the village. So, Crowley went to get the best white horse there. When he came back with the white horse, she told him now to put her sitting up in the horse before himself and to get two swords. She instructed him to place one sword in each hand and to cut them down at each side as fast as the horse would go for they would be in swarms at each side trying to steal her off the horse. This Crowley did, and he cut them down and kept on cutting them down until he had the last one cut down. Then he had the young lady saved. She told him now to drive on as far as three miles and to stop at such a house and this he did. She told him to take her down off the horse and to place her on the ground. She told him that was her father's house, that there was a sick girl inside in the room, and to go to her father and to ask the key of the room door. She told him to tell her father that he was a doctor that he would go to see his daughter, and that he would cure her for him. The father agreed and gave him the key and told him that if he would cure her that he would give him all the gold he wanted. Crowley went into the room and locked the door behind him leaving the father standing outside the door waiting for the glad news of his daughter recovering. He set to work inside the room and went over to the girl's sick bed and took her out of the bed in his arms without delay, placing her on the grate over a blazing fire. She started to scream as loud as she could when he was placing her on the grate. When her father heard the screaming, he ran for his gun and tried to burst in the door to shoot Crowley. At that moment the young lady that was outside the door jumped inside the door and ran to her father and put her arms around him saying, 'O father, father! I am your daughter whom Crowley has saved. Don't shoot him. She was only a spirit that was put there in the bed instead of me when they swept me away. I could not come in beyond the door until he put her out the chimney.' The father ran to Crowley and caught him by the hand and told him that he would give him all his gold and houses belonging to him and to marry his daughter. Crowley got married to the young lady and they all lived happily together after.

Collector: Mary Sullivan
Informant: Mrs. Hannah Mansfield, aged 39

Fionn Mac Cumhail and the Giant

One day Fionn Mac Cumhail's men went to the hill cutting turf. Fionn remained at home minding the house. He went out and looked around him and he saw a big ship coming towards him in the sea. He chewed his finger, and the knowledge he got was that if he was with them that they would be in the better of him for ever, and that if he was not with them that they would not. They landed near the house. Fionn got into the cradle and told his wife to make a cake and to put a griddle in the middle of the cake. Then the man came into the house, and his name was Dub-Gorm. He was a giant. He asked Fionn's wife for something to eat. She gave him the cake, and the first bite he took left all his teeth in it. When he had eaten, he asked what she had in the cradle and she said a baby, and he walked over and put his finger in his mouth, and Fionn bit his finger. The man said he has the teeth and that he might not wear them. He asked her what exercise have the Fianna of Eireann. She said that they had to throw a stone over a house and be to the other side to meet it before it reached the ground. He went out then and he drove all Fionn Mac Cumhail's cattle to the shore and put them into the boat and they got stuck. Fionn asked his wife to go out and see what they were doing, and she told him that they were throwing all the cattle into the boat. Fionn went down to the shore, and they had all the cattle into boat but for the bull. Fionn said that he would not leave them have the bull, and each of them caught a horn of the bull and split the bull in two halves. The men came from the mountain, and he threw them all into the boat and they got stuck to it.

Fionn's youngest son lived in a cell underground. He lived on the marrow of bones. He thought that something was happening at home. When he came home, he came to the shore. They were all inside in the boat and then he and the giant started to fight. The young man could not do anything with the giant for the giant was too strong. They were fighting until they were up to the belly in the water. The boy knocked him in the water and kept him down until he was dead. Fionn chewed his finger, and he got the knowledge that the giant's throat should be cut, and the blood should be spared and kept to rub on everybody in the boat. He had no blood for Connán-Maol. He caught him by the hand, and he pulled him up, but his skin tore, and they had to sew a sheep skin on to him. He had a enough of wool to make a pair of stockings for each of the Finnia of Eireann every year out of the wool that grew on his back side.

Collector: Peggy O Sullivan,
Informant: Michael Guihan, grandfather, aged 83

The Difficult Tasks

Long ago there lived a very poor boy. One day he set out to seek his worth. As he was walking along, he came up towards a big castle where there lived a big giant of a king. On entering the castle, the poor boy told his story to the king. The king gave him a job to do. He told him to clean out the stable and to have it cleaned out for dinner time. If he did not have it cleaned out by dinner, he would kill him. The poor boy went to work and did not know what to do as he could not make any hand of it and the time was drawing near. When he used to throw out a shovel, six shovels more used to come in. At long last when he was worn out, he sat down and did not know what to do. He was full of grief in fear before he would be killed.

Just as dinner time was drawing near, a young lady came up to him and asked him what his trouble was. She took the shovel from his hand and told him to put three strokes of the shovel in the threshold of the door. He did as the young lady told him, and as soon as he did the stable appeared quite clean, so he was delighted to have his job done. When the king came, he asked him did he do it. The boy told him he did so the king said very good. That was the work of one day.

When next morning came the king came to him again and told him that he had another job for him to do. He said that the pony was outside in the field, to go and catch him, and to have him inside for the night in the stable. He went out to carry home the pony, but he failed in catching him, for every time he tried to go near the pony to catch him, he used to run away. He gave the whole day trying to catch him, but it was all in vain. He was that way until coming on night. The young lady came unto him, as she came the time before, and she asked him what was his trouble? He told her that her father had sent him to catch the pony and that he but could not. She gave him a whistle and told him to whistle three times. He did as she told him, and as soon as he did, the pony walked up to him and laid his head down in his breast, so he brought him home and put him into the stable and had him sleep there for the night. Straight after the king came along and asked him had he the pony inside in the stable. The boy said yes. The king was surprised he was able to catch the pony, so he said very good.

The next morning came and the king came to him again and told him that he had another job for him. He told him that if he would be able to do it, he would give him his daughter to marry and his castle to live in. He told him that there was an island three miles out in the ocean. There were bird's eggs there. He was to bring them back to him and to have them inside for his dinner. The poor boy went away to get the eggs. When he went down near the edge of the water, he was surprised to see the big wild ocean before him, and he had no chance of going to the island to get the bird eggs. He sat down in the stream near the edge of the water, lamenting as he did not know what to do. He was not long there when the same young lady came up to him. As before, she asked him what was troubling him. He told her that the king had sent him to bring back the eggs but that he had no chance of reaching the island by the wild rough sea. The young lady told him to cut off the tops of his ten fingers and that she would make a ladder. He did as she told him. The ladder reached from the shore to into the island. He walked across on the ladder to the island through the wild ocean and came back with the eggs to the king for his dinner. The king seeing what he had done was very much surprised and could not put any further tasks to him. He took him into his palace and told him that he would give him his daughter to marry the next day.

When the next day came, the boy took the young lady to the church with him to get married. They entered the church, and they went up to the altar. Just as the priest was starting the ceremony and the couple were going to be bound as husband and wife, a big black dog walked in the door and up through the chapel towards the altar, caught hold of the young lady, and took her away out in his mouth. There could be no trace seen of her for ever after. The poor boy was left there standing by himself wondering what had happened. He had to go away his road, poor as ever again.

Collector: Mary O Sullivan
Informant: Mrs Hannah Mansfield, mother, aged 39

Two Sisters

Long ago, in the time of the famine, there lived in a house in Adrigole two sisters. I don't know their names. One day they were nearly dying with the hunger. They came across the mountains to Glenmore. When they were just in sight of Glenmore, one of them gave up there with the hunger. The other one kept going away till she came to a house. That was my grandmother's house. She was nearly dead, but she ate there, and she got ill again. She stayed there for the night, but she never thought of her sister when herself was alright. She thought of her in the morning but when she went to see her, she was dead. The fields and mountains were white with frost. She is buried at a place called Claídhe na Teóram. Some people used to say prayers when they used pass that way. There was one man there who used to say prayers all the time, but he is dead now.

Collector: Patrick OSullivan

The Member of St Joseph's Union

Years ago, a woman who returned from America took rooms in Miss O'Brien's of Castletown. She liked to live there. Her husband and two children were dead. She felt unwell and sent to New York for a younger sister to care for her.

One morning an old man dressed like a tradesman walked into the Cannon's Hall. He asked the housekeeper was a priest in as there was a person dying in St Joseph's Boat. She said there was and went to call a priest who was in his room. The priest told her tell the messenger wait. When she came back the man was gone. She ran out and asked the men who worked on the lawn to call the man, they told her they saw him pass in, but he did not come out. A lot of fishing boats were in the harbour at the time drying their nets. The priest got the men to row him to St Joseph's boat. After searching, there was no boat of that name or no man sick. The priest told them he would go to the town and inquire, and they could row back again and try and find out who could be sick. After enquiring, the priest was on his way home. After passing Miss O'Brien's he stood and looked out at the boats and said in a low voice, "A is person dying and a priest is here." That very moment he heard a rush in the stairs and a woman shouting, "A Priest, a Priest." He ran in and was told the old lady was dying, she was conscious but very weak. She made her peace with God and told them all she was a member of St Joseph's Union, and the patron of a happy death never forgot her.

Collector: Rita O'Shea
Informant: Mrs Julia O'Shea, grandmother, aged 67

The Best Dog

Long ago there was a sheepdog at the post office in Ardea. He was supposed to be the best dog in the parish. At one time there was a football march between Ardea and Durrus. In the sliabh near Clonee bridge they played. The ball very often was kicked out in the lake. The dog used swim out for it without anyone telling him.

At one time they missed a horse. He was bought from a man from Cloherane. The horse left Ardea in the night and went to Cloherane next day. They went searching for the animal At length, they told the dog to go and find him. The dog went on with a number of the family, and never stopped until he came to Cloherane mountain, and high up there he got the horse. He used to go to meet the car coming from town, and he used to know the noise of it. One night one of the boys lost a rug, the dog was behind the car and brought the rug with him in his mouth home. He lived fourteen years. His name was Shep.

Informant: Jeremiah Sullivan Gloss, Lehid

How his Brother's Death was Revealed to a Soldier

Long ago there was a man living in Mayo. His brother was a soldier in the British army. He was called to go to war but when he was training, he got hurt. He was in hospital four months. He got better again and went training again. After a few days his brother called him home. The night before, as he put his loaded gun away, it went off. In the morning the officer asked for his gun. When the soldier found the shot gone off and drops of blood on the floor. He did not say a word about the shot being gone off. When he reached home his brother was found shot near a ditch. The brother was laid out when he came home and the house full of people. The second night of the wake when they were saying the rosary, they heard a noise saying, "Níl an fear sin marbh in aon chor ach tá sé 'na colath go sám [That man is not dead at all but he is in a state of peace]," and that minute the dead man woke up. The people say that it was his ghost that was lying there in the bed.

Collector: Daniel Gallivan
Informant: Mrs O' Shea, aged 80, weaver, Ardea, Co. Kerry

Kate Merwick of Coulagh Ard

Over twenty years ago a girl lived in Coulagh Ard named Kate Merwick. When she was a little girl, her mother died. On All Soul's Day, about eighteen years after her mother dying, she was cooking the dinner when she saw a woman standing on the floor. The woman asked her did she know her. She said she did not. She told the girl that she could not know her for she was her mother who died when she was very young. She told her daughter that she was in purgatory for eighteen years and to get a mass said for her, and then her purgatory would be, over and then she disappeared.

Collector: Thomas Harrington, Drombohilly
Informant: Mary Harrington, mother, aged 39

An Ardea Fortune Teller

Long ago, the girls in this parish used believe in having their fortune told to know what way of living their husbands would have, or would they ever get married. There was a house which is now no longer there at Ardea, west of the post office, and the old woman in that house would tell fortunes. The way she used tell was to get seven saucers and place them in a row on the table. On the first saucer there was a few grains of oats, on the second money, on the third water, on the fourth earth, on the fifth a red rag, on the sixth a blue rag, and the seventh was empty. The person who would want try would be blind folded. The saucers would be mixed from their position. The girl would be led to the table and whatever saucer she would put her fingers into would tell her the kind of living her husband would have. The oats meant a farmer, money meant a rich man, water to go to America, earth a sudden death, a red rag a soldier, a blue rag a policeman, and seventh meant a spinster. The old woman's name was Joan Sullivan the piper.

Collector: Patrick Sullivan
Informant: Patsy Sullivan, aged 73

The First Black Cow

The first black cow came to Ireland long ago. The people believed in fairies, and there were no black cows in Ireland, but all red and white. One of the white cows went away from the fairies, and a farmer got her. The farmer kept the cow and she had two calves. The farmer said he would kill the cow. The butcher and all were there. The butcher was just going to strike the cow when he heard a loud noise, and the cow flew away. The calves never heard the noise, but they turned black with fright. One of the calves was a bull and the other a heifer, and that is how the first black cow came to Ireland.

Collector: Neil O' Sullivan
Informant: Paddy Shea, aged 79

The Plucked Hen

Once upon a time there lived an old woman and an old man in an old house. The old woman used be always talking about death and wishing to die. One day the old man went and plucked a hen and left her go again. He went into the house then and he and his wife sat near the fire. He wasn't long there when the plucked hen walked in the door. The old woman was the first to see her, and she got frightened and she said to the old man, "Cad é sin ag teacht isteach an doras. [What is that coming in the door?]". "O", said the old man, "Sin é an bás. [That is death]." The old woman got frightened, and she ran. From that day off she never spoke of death.

Collector: Annie Leary, Ardea, Co. Kerry
Informant: Mrs Tim Leary, mother, aged 49

The Jealous Farmers

There were three neighbours living near each other and two of them were jealous of the other man. He had a fine bullock and they said they would kill his bullock he had for ploughing to keep him down. They grabbed the animal and the man skinned him and brought him to town to sell the hide. When he was going to the town it was raining so he turned the hide inside out towards the rain. The birds were perching on it, and he caught a raven. He sold the hide for ten shillings, and he kept the raven. He went into a public house and asked for a glass of whiskey. He pinched the bird he had under his coat, and the bird made a noise. The barmaid asked what he had, and he said he had a bird that had knowledge, and that it was telling him she had better whiskey in another bottle. She said she had and that the bird was right. She gave him the good whiskey. The girl asked him would he sell the bird. He said he would not like to part with it unless he got a lot of money for him. She said she would give him £20 for the raven. He sold the bird for £20 and went home. The men asked how much did he get for the hide. He said £20. They did not believe him, but he showed them the £20. It was the money of the raven he showed them. They went home, killed their own bullocks, and brought the hides to the market where they sold them for six shillings. They were mad because their fine bullocks were gone. They said they would kill the cheating farmer.

The farmer was sleeping with his mother in the bed. He put his mother in the bottom of the bed where he used to sleep himself. This night the two men rushed in the window and killed his mother. They thought it was himself they had. They left her there. He went and buried his mother. When he came home, he told the two men there was a great price for old women in town for making gun powder. They went home and killed their own mothers and brought them to the market and they were up and down the town all day long. The guards heard they were there, and they told them go and bury the bodies. They said they would kill him fair or foul.

They caught him on a mountain one day and put him into a bag. When they were passing a field, they saw a lame hare crossing the field and went after it. When they were gone a man with a lot of cattle was passing and he saw the bag moving and he ran down. "What are you doing there?" he said, "I am going to be drowned in a lake and that is heaven". The man said, "put me into the bay, they won't know who it is because I would like to go to heaven". The farmer in the bag asked what the man would give him if he swapped places. The man said he would give him all the cattle he was driving. The farmer left the man in the bag and drove home the cattle. Afterwards they came and put the bag into the lake. Next day he met the two farmers again, and they asked him how did he like the lake. He told them heaven was in the bottom of the lake, and that there was plenty of everything there. He told them that he got all the cattle there and more if he wanted them. He told them everything was free there. They said one of them would go down and get what he wanted. One of them went down and he was never heard or seen since. The other man had to stay quiet then.

Informant: Mike MacCarthy, aged 63, Bunaw, Co. Kerry

A Sign after Death

There lived a man in Lehud long ago named Donal Fan. His father died. Every Spring after he was buried, a spirit would appear to Donal and tell him what field to till. Donal thought it was his father's spirit that used to come to him. He told the priest about it. The priest told him that next time he'd come, to have a bottle of holy water in his pocket without any cork, and when he would see the spirit, to throw it at him. He told him also that if it was his father's spirit that it would stand, and if it was another spirit that it would go away. That night he waited until the spirit came. He threw the holy water at it. It was an evil spirit that used to come to him.

Séan Ruadh

Long ago a robber lived about five miles from Killarney at a place called the Robber's Den. His name was Séan Ruadh. He was a very cruel man who had a gun and used kill a great deal of people and rob them. He had a great crock of gold.

One day he was riding on a horse going home to his den. He saw a beautiful lady and caught her and put her before him on the saddle. He brought her home and kept her to get married to her. One day he went into a public house and a great deal of people were inside, and when they saw him, they got frightened and ran except one brave man. The robber went to the man and went looking ugly at him. He told him to go away from him. "If you won't, I won't long be putting you away," he said. He told the lad that he was a robber, and that he killed a great deal of people. "Well," said the lad, "you did not kill me yet and I am not afraid of you." He asked the lad would he be his man. He said he would, and the robber asked him could he use a gun. The lad couldn't so he said, "I will learn you to do so." The boy was able to use a gun.

The robber brought him home showed him his den and the pot of gold, but not the place he had the girl in. The girl was the man's sister. The robber started to show the man how to use a gun. When he gave the gun to the lad, he stood out from him and left a shot at him wounding one of his legs. He made him kneel down before him and stay there until he would return. He went and got the pot of gold and filled his pockets with it and left out his sister. The robber told the lad not to kill himself and that he could have all the gold. He drove the robber out of the place as far as a place called Glenflesk. He gave some of the money to the poor people. It was that man that hunted the robber out of that place.

Collector: Patrick Sullivan, Lehid, Co. Kerry
Informant: Jeremiah O' Sullivan, father, aged 57

Jackie Shea from Ardtully

There was a gentleman lived near Kilgarvan in a place called Ardtully. His name was Mr Orpen. He lived in a fine castle. One of his sons, Mr Hugh, was very popular with the people. He was a tall handsome man and he used be walking along the road from Ardtully to Kilgarvan every day. His steward bought a milk cow from an old man about two miles from the castle. He paid a good price for her, and the man was very pleased. He asked the man could he get anyone to drive the cow to the castle the next day. The old man said he could, that Jackie Shea will drive her, and that he is a real honest boy and won't hurt her going. Tell him to have her at the castle about ten o'clock. The man said he would. Next morning Jackie started with the cow. It was hard to bring her but Jackie having no shoes on him was driving her the best way he could. About a half a mile from the castle the cow got very cross. He met a man on the road. The cow was going in a gap. He asked the man would he please stop the cow. The man did and walked along the road with Jackie to the castle. He asked Jackie where was he going with the cow. Jackie said to the castle; "if you will help me to drive her as far as the gate, I will give you half of what I will get inside." "How do you know you will get anything said the man?" "I do well said Jackie. Nobody ever went in there but was well paid for his trouble." "May be," said the man, "after waiting for you to come out you would not give me half of what you get?" "I will sir," said Jackie. "I would not tell you a lie for the price of a cow." The gate was opened, and Jackie drove in the cow. The man was Mr Orpen. He went in a near way to the castle. He told the butler to give Jackie his dinner. He told him to give him two pairs of boots, and he gave the butler a sovereign to give to Jackie. Jackie was invited to the dinner. He thanked him for it, he told him he was in a hurry that there was a man waiting for him at the gate. But to give him a piece of bread and meat, the boots and the money. Out with him to the gate and the man was outside before him. "I hope I did not keep you two long waiting," said Jackie. "You did not." said the man. "You got something?" "O! I did." said Jackie.

"I got one shilling and two pair of boots and two parcels of bread and meat." Jackie gave the shilling to the man and told him give him a sixpence back, he also gave him the large pair of boots and one parcel of bread and meat. He asked him was he sure it was a shilling he got inside. Jackie said yes. The man asked him would he know the man that gave it to him. He said he would. He brought Jackie to the castle. Jackie pointed out the man. The man admitted giving a shilling. He sacked the butler and kept Jackie in his place for years after.

Collector: Patrick O' Sullivan, Lehid, Co. Kerry
Informant: Jeremiah Sullivan, father, aged 57

A Mermaid Horse

In Rinn Beg near Dingle there lived a family of Flahertys. One day a strange horse came in by the tide. He was a brown horse with a black tail. He had a collar of his own. The Flahertys saw him coming in and landing on the strand. They kept him and he worked for them, he ploughed and drew loads for them.

One day they were going ploughing with him. Before ploughing they were stowing out a loft, they put the collar outside the door. When the horse saw the collar, he put his head into it and ran away to the sea. The Flaherty's followed him as far as the sea. They saw him going southwest out the mouth of Dingle Bay. That mermaid horse worked seven years with the Flahertys.

Collector: Tim Brosnan, Daingean Uí Chúis, Co. Kerry

The Kilmoe Mermaid

There is a graveyard in the farthest back place in Ireland by the name of Kilmoe. There was a man living in that place. The man was standing on a rock near the sea after being fishing. A mermaid appeared to him. She had the finest hair he ever saw on any person. He stole the cloak from her, and she had to follow him, then he kept her for seven years. She told him not to ever invite a landlord to his house, and not to ever tell a story to a priest or to bring a story from him. She said not to ever sell a polly cow nor to buy a polly cow, but not to ever be without a polly cow. He was setting nets and the cloak went in the sea, and she got the cloak, and she went away.

A Mermaid

The Mermaid is one of the deep-sea creatures nearly related to the seal. The seal is of a smaller species and lives nearer to the shore. The Mermaid's body and head resemble that of a woman, as do her two hands which she sometimes uses as legs as she has none, but a tail like a fish. When seen by mariners in the ocean it denotes a coming storm and they prepare for it, but when convenient to the shore they consider it a bad omen. Years ago, a man who lived in Bere Island used often see a mermaid in the strand combing her beautiful hair. By night he used hear her moaning and caoning like the banshee. One day he was fishing in the bay with other men. He saw the mermaid not far away. They made for the shore, but the waves got furious, and their boat was dashed to pieces on the rocks. The man who saw the mermaid was drowned the others clung to the rocks and were saved. The strand is called Craíg na Muiteeg and the rock is Faill na d'tadg.

Collector: Rita O' Shea, Drombohilly Lower, Co. Kerry
Informant: Julia O' Shea, grandmother, aged 67

LEHID
People, Places and Property

Den O'Sullivan the Piper

There was an old piper named Den O'Sullivan. His son named Jim O'Sullivan lives in Kenmare now. Den Sullivan used to go to different places and build a little hut for himself and his wife near the road. The landlord didn't want any of those poor huts to be seen. He used to try and get the hut down, but to pay the old man. The old man would then go away and build another hut. He kept doing that some time until he couldn't build any more for the police were put on his track and he got too old to make a house or to be travelling. He went to the pattern at Bunaw and he brought the pipes. When he was coming home, there was stepping-stones to cross and he missed his step, and he fell into the river, and he fell on the pipes and they began to play.

Collector: James Harrington, Ardea, Co. Kerry
Informant: Mary Sheehan, aged 81

Murty Larry

Murty Larry lived in Drombohilly. He was a poet and a carpenter. He was clever but poor. It was he who roofed Lauragh church. One day he got a letter from the priest of Adrigole to go over there to roof a church. He left on a Sunday evening a d crossed the mountains east to Bunawn. He left Bunawn the following morning and crossed the Bunawn mountains to go to Adrigole. On his way a shower came, and he went into a schoolhouse for shelter. The school master was inside and when he saw Murty he said, "Isn't it far away the Kerry ravens come to fly for shelter." Murty answered him back and said, "They come to wet their beaks in the shorn sheep of the Macarty Caoraig", because the schoolteacher's name was Macarty. They used call his father the Macarty caoraig.

Collector: Julia Harrington
Informant: Tom Harrington, father aged 65

The Parish Clerk

Long ago there was a man named Michael ["Micky the Clerk"] Sullivan who lived at Ardea. He was employed by the parish priest, Father Barrett. He had no learning. The priest got suddenly sick on Sunday morning. Michael was sent to Lauragh Church to tell the people that the priest was sick, and they would have no Mass. It was about twelve o'clock when he arrived with a horse and a side car. He told the Clerk, Charles MacCarthy, to tell the people that they would have not Mass today. "I will not tell them," Said Charles, "tell them yourself." Michael stood up on the pillar of the gate and all the people gathered around him. Michael said, "My dear people of Lauragh and Ardea, the priest got sick, we will not have no Mass today. I would advise ye to go into the Church and say y'er prayers, go home quietly, avoid evil and do good." Well, said John Larry, "It is as good a sermon as I ever heard."

Collector: Patrick Sullivan, Lehid, Co. Kerry
Informant: Jeremiah Sullivan, father, aged 57

Dr Maybury's Servant and the Holy Well

Years ago, when Dr Maybury lived near Sound bridge, Kenmare, one of his servants was from Tuosist. She was a very good maid and used always milk the morning and evening. Once she got a wart in her face. The doctor's medicine or ointment was of no benefit. It was very sore. She dreamt to go to a holy well in Bunane to perform rounds and wash the sore with the water. She prepared to go there on the following Saturday evening and should go there again on Sunday morning. It happened one of the doctor's cows had warts on her udder which were very sore, and she was very cross when milking her. Mrs Maybury was a protestant and questioned the maid when she returned Saturday evening. She said that the maid had faith and thought she would get cured. She asked would she bring a bottle with her next morning and bring some water home and sprinkle some on the cow's udder. The maid could not refuse. So that night she slept very little and prayed to have God direct her as her Mrs was a protestant. Next morning, she went off and took her bottle and was afraid to fill it with water from the well. When coming back, she filled it with water from the roadside. She washed the cow, and the warts were all gone next day, and her own face was cured also. She was afterwards Mrs Harrington in Derryloughy and she told the story to my grandmother.

Collector: Rita O Shea
Informant: Julia O Shea, grandmother, aged 67

Daniel O'Connell

Daniel O Connell lived in Caherciveen. The old ruin is still there. Ivy is growing up the wall and a big elder tree is growing a long side of it. There was a bit of poetry made about him. One day Daniel was passing a shop in London and up on the glass was written.

> In this beehive we're all alive
> And whiskey makes us funny
> If you are dry come in and try
> The flavour of our honey.

Daniel's answer was:

> In this beehive we're all alive.
> And whiskey makes us funny
> If you are dry come in and try
> The flavour of our honey
> If I went in the bees would sting
> Because I have no money.

Collector: Neil O Sullivan, Bunaw, Co. Kerry
Informant: Mrs Mary O Sullivan, mother, age 44

Hedge Schools

The principal school in Lauragh was built in the Millionaire's land. There used be forty scholars going there. The name of the teacher was Seánaín Báille. If there were four scholars going to school, they would give four shillings to join. They used learn Irish and catechism. The master used eat in every second house. He used eat potatoes and butter for his meals. The school was divided in two parts. There were two shoemakers in one part. One day one shoemaker gave the scholars a piece of wax. The boys then put it on the chair that the master used to have. When the master sat down it got stuck to his trousers. The scholars were fighting, and he got up to stop them. He made a great rush down and he carried the chair tied to him. All the fellows got a great fit of laughing. He got out his penknife and said that if he found out who did it, he would stab him through the heart. He never found out who did it. When he used get into a temper he used call them a pack of hungry foxes. He used to have a basket and he used be going around selling jotters and used be selling lead pencils at a halfpenny each.

Collector: Dan Gallivan
Informant: Mrs Shea, aged 76, weaver, Ardea, Co. Kerry

Lauragh Church

Lauragh Church was built over seventy years ago. When it was roofed, a great storm came and blew off the roof. It had to be roofed over again. The men that did the carpentry work in it were my great-grand-uncle, Morty Larry, and my great-great-grandfather Ned Jones. My grandfather remembers being at mass in the old Church. There was a gallery in it.

Collector: Anna Sullivan
Informant: Michael Guihan, grandfather, aged 82

LEHID
Farming, Trade and Crafts

Hens and Hatching

The best kind of eggs to set are round eggs. The best kind of a hen to set is a hen about a year old. The best day to set a hen is Wednesday and the best time of the day is at nightfall. A great sign to have a stranger come is to see two hens fighting. When the tide is ebbing, it is the best time to put a hen hatching. When you hear a hen clucking it is a sign of rejoicing. When you see hen's biting themselves it is a sign of rain.

Collector: Patrick O' Sullivan, Lehid, Co. Kerry
Informant: Paddy Moriarty, Dawros, Co. Kerry

Old Trades

The cost of a pair of shoes long ago was fifteen shillings. The shoemaker in Lehud was John Leary. The cost of an apprenticeship was ten pounds for three years. A set of horseshoes would cost two shillings; a gate, fifteen shillings; a harrow, twenty-two; a bawn spade, half a crown; a crane, fifteen; and a candlestick, a shilling. A plough was five pounds.

Limekilns were very plentiful long ago. There was one below the bridge of Lehud. One in Cuan a gCoilleach, one above near Dan Shea the bakers, and one near the sound wood. The limestone used be got over in Blackwater. It used be carried over by boat. It used be burned by turf.

Collector: Daniel Gallivan, Ardea, Co. Kerry
Informant: Patrick Gallivan, father, aged 60

Killing Animals

Long ago the old people used'nt throw away any part of the cow they used kill but the small instestines, and the white liver which they called the lights. When they used kill her, they'd cut her skin and open her. Then they used take out the stomach, the máilín a leabhair, the máilín a páircheanna, and the puddings. Then they used gather all the tallow together for the purpose of making candles and sráthlógs. When the interior parts were cold, someone used carry them to a stream and clean and wash them. The legs were then cut off from the hide and turned into various uses. Some people used tie the four legs together and hang them on a nail in the chimney and keep them for luck. Other people kept a part of an ear for luck. Some people used skin the legs put them into a pot and boil them. The sráthlógs were made from old calico dipped in the melted tallow and rolled together from each side. They are then left harden and used.

Collector: Annie Leary, Ardea
Informant: Mrs Tim Leary, aged

A Forge

There was an old forge in Lehid in Dan Sullivan's farm. It was in the field below the house, west of the lane in the Field of the Cocks. It belonged to an old smith named Séan Gaba. He was a grandfather of Dan Sullivan. He used to shoe horses and wheels and a great number of more different work besides.

The instruments the smiths use are the hammer, nails, pincers, anvil, and nippers used for grooving irons. The tub of water the smith has for cooling the iron is called the tóisk, which means a dam or a stopped locáns, the smiths used to cool the iron and they call it the tóisk ever since. There was another old forge in the bottom of our land north. I don't know who owned it. The field is called after it Carcsin. The foundation is there yet near a stream. It was near that forge my father found a battle axe when he was cutting the turf.

Collector: Thomas Harrington

LEHID
Local Customs

Death and signs of death

When a person is sick it said that it is a sign of death when they hold up their hands looking at them or if their mouth gets drawn. Sometimes if a person with good hearing is dying, he loses it, or if a person with bad hearing was dying, he'd get good hearing before he dies. People who die outside are never brought into the dwelling house. The soap, towel and water that washes a corpse are never used again. They are thrown away. When a child or father is dying, all the people of the house go out, only the mother stays. The corpse isn't touched for about an hour after death. It is then taken from the bed and washed. The two ends of the bed are covered with white sheets. A white sheet and spread are put under a corpse in the bed. There is a long dress called a habit put on the dead body. Long ago the old people wouldn't leave anyone cry until the corpse was laid out. The clock is stopped when the person is dying. The cock crows mournfully while the person is sick. There are no pipes or tobacco given at the first child's wake.

Collector: Annie Leary
Informant: Mrs Tim Leary, mother, aged 49, Ardea

At a Person's Death

To know that a person is dead to stick a needle in his skin if the hole closes, he is alive if the hole remains, he is dead. When you are laying out a person you should not cry, for the soul has to go through a narrow path near hell and the devil has big dogs in guard to snap the soul. Crying wakes the dogs. It is said that it is not right to cry while laying the person.

Collector: Patrick O' Sullivan
Informant: John Healy

Wearing the Clothes

It is the custom that when a person dies, a friend or relation of the dead person will wear their clothes for three Sundays in order that the person that dies will have them in the next world. At sunset on the Saturday evening after the person is buried, the woman of the house puts out the clothes on the back of a chair. The person that is going to wear them will come, call the person that is dead and say, "Come here and take your clothes for God's sake, or else give them to me and I will wear them for you". After that the person will wear them three Sundays.

Collector: Mary Casey, Lehid, Co. Kerry
Informant: Mrs P. Casey, aged 49

Old Sayings about Marriage

It is said that it is unlucky for a wedding party to meet a funeral on their way home from the church or going to church. It is also said to be unlucky to lose or forget the ring. Long ago a man, Darby Hartnett from Leanfie, lost the ring on his way to the church to be married. The priest said not to mind going trying for it, but he formed a ring out of a blade of straw and married them with the ring made of the blade of straw as a wedding ring.

Collector: Mary Shea, Lehid, Co. Kerry
Informant: Patrick Shea, father, aged 40

Old Sayings

Once upon a time a man from Adrigole was praising the hens how they were so strong there. He said they used take the cake of bread of the table. A very good sign of the housekeeper said the other man.

A poor man was walking along the road one day and he met a priest and a curate. He took off his hat and asked them both for alms. The parish priest put his hand in his pocket and gave him two shillings. The poor man said, "God bless you Father." The curate put his hand in his pocket and gave him half a crown. The poor man said, "God almighty bless you Father." The poor man went a few paces and the parish priest called after him and asked him, "What is the difference between God bless you and God almighty bless you?" and the poor man said, "sixpence father."

Informant: Peter Healy, aged 68

LEHID
Natural World and Weather Lore

A Whirlwind

Whirlwinds are very common in glens. They do a lot of harm. It is two balls of air that strike together in the mountains and sweep down through the lowlands. There is a blast in it, and you should go a side when it is passing because you might get a sore leg or hand.

There were two men travelling through the wood back of the schoolhouse of Glenmore. They heard a great noise, and they did not know what it was. They saw the branches of a big tree bend down to the ground near them by a whirlwind. They were struck with terror. They took off their hats and blessed themselves. It was a very calm day.

Collector: John Healy
Informant: Pat Healy, father, aged 52

A Story About Thunder and Lightning

One night about twenty years ago there was a great thunder storm. Lightning got into a house in Fehanaugh of a man by the name of Denis O'Sullivan. It knocked the chimney, broke a board in the dresser. There were two bottles in the dresser, a bottle of Holy Water and a bottle of oil. The bottle of oil was broken, and the bottle of Holy Water was not touched. The lightning broke the door and dug a big hole in the fence outside the door and knocked a cock of hay. The people of the house got a great fright.

Collector: Peggy O Sullivan
Informant: Nancy O Sullivan, grandmother, aged 80

Lehid
Sea and Shipwrecks

Trammel Fishing and its Preparations

First you must buy the thread called hemp. Then you get small square pieces of timber called macesticks to twist the thread around them. Then you will get a long piece of timber about half a foot in length and about an inch in breadth to make a beating needle out of it. Then get a long piece of thread in on it. First you will knot the thread around the macestick and beat on the meshes until you have thirty-eight meshes in depth. You will keep on beating it until you have thirty-six fathoms in length. Then you will have to get tar and boil it in an old pot. When it is boiled, you will have to put a board over the pot and make a hole in the middle of the board and put the trammel into the pot of tar and pull it up through the hole of the board. When it is taken out and tarred there will have to be a rope put along one side of it called the foot rope, and then a cork rope to the other side of it to keep up the trammel on the water from sinking to the deep when it is set in the water. Then when it is completed, you would get a boat and five men, everyone is to have his own trammel, and board them in with stones and a rope tied to the anchor out of the trammels. Then when they have them boarded, they take them away out to the deep sea where there would be any prospects in catching a good haul of hake or pollock. They would have them set a day and a night and then they used to go out and haul them into the boat. Some of them used to have up to eighty or ninety. Other days some used to have up to sixty and some more up to forty and so on. Sometimes when they used to be starting out for sea it used to be very nice and calm, and them when they used to be hauling them it used to get very rough and rise to a high storm. Then they should throw them out back into the sea and row in for safety to the nearest landing place to the north shore and stay there until it calmed.

One day they went out setting them and when they were half ways out one of the crew seen a white horse in the water not far from land, but he never told it to any one of the crew and no other one saw it only the one man. All went well until they went out to where the trammels were set.

Then when they went to haul them out, they had only three hauls made when they saw the boat sinking. The water was up to the gunnel of the boat and all the men got very much excited and they did not know what to do. Some of them cut the laces of their boots so when the boat would be drowning, they would try and swim to land. Some more of them thought of throwing out the trammels back into the sea. When they were putting them out some of the crew saw something strange tangled in one of the trammels, which resembled a glove. When they were put back out into the sea, the boat was rising by degrees until it came to its normal height in the water. Then they pulled to shore and put the one man that seen the white horse out to shore as he was near fainting in the boat. They rowed out again and brought the trammels in, so they bought them for good and did not go out anymore. The names of the men that were there that day were John Riney and his son Dan, and Daniel Riney of Clonee, Dan Downing, my uncle Patrick O'Sullivan, and Patsy Galvan of Ardea. Daniel Riney, now dead, was the man that saw the white horse a little distance from his own boat and it appeared again at the middle of the bay. All the crew could have seen the mirage that happened on that day and concerning the image of the glove it appeared just like one real glove. When the boat was sinking there were any amount of fish floating on the top of the water around the boat.

Collector: Mary Sullivan, Leaghillaun, Co. Kerry
Informant: Patrick O' Sullivan, aged 63

Seine Fishing Long Ago

Seine fishing was a very profitable occupation in our harbour when herrings and mackerel were plentiful. There used be a crew of sixteen men in every seine engaged at the fishing from August to November, every night except Sunday night during the dark moon. There would be ten in the seine boat which carried the seine, and six men in the other boat which was called the follower. The men in the seine boat would throw a rope to the man in the stem of the follower. That rope was called the warp and it was attached to the end of the seine. The man in the stern of the seine boat was the hewer and it was by his directions the seine would be set around the shoal of fish. When they would have the fish surrounded the men in the seine boat would then proceed to take the foot from the net which was carried out by a rope called the lanquar, pulled through two sheaves weighted down by two half hundred weights. The follower would tie the rope called the warp on the boat and pull in the opposite way to the seine boat so that they would not fall in over the net which they were pursuing it because it was in the purse of the net the fish would be caught.

Fishermen are as a rule very superstitious, for instance under any condition would any three persons be allowed to light their pipes with one match. It was also counted very unlucky to figure the amount of fish in a shoal before it was netted.

Trawling

Trawling means fishing with the beam trawl which is a triangular bag like net towed along the sea bottom. The mouth of the trawl is attached to a frame consisting of a long wooden beam supported by a triangular hoop of iron at each end. As the net is towed along the ground fish are disturbed and rise above the foot rope and are prevented from escaping by the upper side of the net. They are swept into its narrow end where their escape is more difficult. The size of the trawl varies according to the size of the vessel working it, but for deep sea fishing the beam is 36 to 50 feet long, and the mesh of the net is always about 4 ins at the mouth to 1 ½ inches at the cod-end. The trawl is towed by means of two bridles which are long ropes of equal length attached one to each trawl head, and a very strong thick rope - the warp - the end of which is fastened by a shackle to the two bridles. The principal fish caught in the trawl are sole, plaice, brill, turbot, cod, pollock, whiting, lemon sole, white sole, witches, eels, dogfish, rays, jellyfish, dory, and ling.

It was in 1896 my grandfather got the first boat. The price he paid for her was £55, The name of the boat was Halcyon. She was bought in Crookhaven, Co Cork where she was a tender to the Fastnet lighthouse.

Collector: Kathleen Downing

The Lehid Seine of Long Ago

The Lehid Seine of long ago as described by Philip Casey to his daughter Mary. There was a seine in Lehid. Every night when they would come in, they would pull the boat up at Caonfie harbour. They would take out the seine and spread it in the field until the next night. The length of the seine was about eighty or ninety fathoms, and it was ten or eleven fathoms deep. Every morning when the men would get the seine and take it to the boat and shove the boat down to the water. Then they would board the seine. The cork rope would be on one side, and the foot rope on the other, coiled nice and carefully. Every man would get into his place and catch his oar.

At the harvest time there would be a light on the water when the fish would rise to the surface, and they would be seen very plainly. At the front of the seine boat a man stood lookout for them. When he would see the fish he would give orders to the captain to get ready. The captain would throw a rope to a man on the follower. It was tied on one end of the seine. That man would give orders to pull up the boat so as to put it under way. He would give orders to the men on the stern to throw out the seine. The seine boat would pull away and make a good wide circle so as to surround the fish. Often the man on the front would peg stones outside the fish. The seine boat is coming up in full sweep to take the other end of the seine from the follower. The seine boat would have the two ends of the seine. As quick as lighting a man on the follower would give a rope to a man on the seine boat. That rope was called the hold on, it was tied to the middle taught. The follower would pull out to keep the seine boat off the seine. They would start to haul the seine and fish in. When they would have a good share of the thread on, they would rip up the hold on then, and tell the follower to come around and take in the cork. They would dry up the thread into the seine boat so as to lift up the fish, and throw it into the follower. Then the remainder if any, would be put into the seine boat.

Collector: George Harrington, Drombohilly Lower, Co. Kerry
Informant: George Harrington

Fair or Foul

Jeremiah McCarthy and his brother Flor of Ardea were two great oarsmen. They used win every race. No other oarsmen used like them. Once two men from Ardgroom were winning all the races and the McCarthys were getting afraid of them because they were thinking they would be beaten. There was going to be a regatta in Bunaw the following Sunday. The two men from Ardgroom came east to ask them to pull against them. Jeremiah was a very cranky fellow and he hated to be beaten in a race. He gave them the dinner before they left. They had fish and potatoes for dinner. The fish was bad and after they going home they got very sick, and the following Sunday they could not get up so the McCarthys won that day.

Collector: Daniel Gallivan, Ardea, Co. Kerry
Informant: Patrick Gallivan, father, aged 60

A Disaster at Sea

One day there were a number of men hauling trammels near Cannaig a h-Éadacháin in Kenmare Bay. A storm arose and all the men were drowned except one man whose name was Pat Sullivan Bates of Ardea. He was born with a cap on his head which was known as a cawl. The old people believe that anyone who was born with a cawl would never be drowned. When the rest of the men were drowned, he stayed on the keel of the boat until another boat came to the rescue.

Collector: Annie Leary

Net Fishing in Kenmare Bay

Net fishing was much more popular long ago than it is now. There are different nets for different kinds of fish. Kenmare River was a noted place for fishing herring some years gone by. My grandfather in Dawrus was a great herring-net fisher. Herring nets are always fished in bright moon because in the dark moon there is light in the water and the herring can see the net. The light is called barsoish. The net is boarded into the boat. On one side there are corks, and a rope all along it to keep it from sinking. On the other side there are little pieces of strings along the net called squinces, and these squinces are stones to sink the net. The herring always go together in shoals. The best place for net fishing is at Ganive near Callerus and Béal-Cáig outside Hillah. Béal-Cáig is a very lonesome place. My grandfather was often made lonesome at Béal-Cáig. He used to hear anchors haul and whistling near him but could not see nothing. He used to pull up his own anchor and clear home. One night he saw a man lifting up his head, pull it down again. It is said that he looked up to see what way the wind was. On another night he saw a big blaze in his own field, and he looked the next morning, and he saw nothing.

A Local Sea Disaster

There was a boat going from Newport to Limerick with a cargo of coal. There were two hundred and fifty tons of coal in the boat. The owner of the boat was from Arklow. His name was Captain Kearns. He had eight men in the boat with him. It was a three masted vessel. She ran into Sneem harbour for shelter in bad weather. It was very stormy, and a high sea was raging. She remained in Sneem harbour that night. In the morning she was blown out of Sneem harbour and was put up on builig. Her sails were torn, and she was holed. They were trying to get Kenmare before she would sink. Some of the men said they would go into Kilmakillogue harbour for safety, but the captain said they would be in Kenmare. They were up outside Blackwater, east of the Maiden rock when she sank. There was no one drowned because they had a lifeboat, and they went into it. The boat was seen going down from Lehid school.

Collector: Bergie O' Sullivan

Lehid
History and Archaeology

Large Stones

In James Sullivan's Larry's mountains there is a number of long stones standing. There are six feet or more high, and two feet wide and two feet thick. There is another stone standing near Jimmy's house, and another where Morty Larry's house was. If you visit one stone, you can see the whole of them. A man that was out from the land commission told Jimmy's father that they were some place of worship.

Collector: Patrick Sullivan
Informant: Margaret Sullivan, mother, aged 45

LEHID
Songs

On the Cooling Shades of Lauragh

The song Murty Larry made for the football game that was played between the Ardea team and the Castlebere team in olden times

On the cooling shades of Lauragh,
it was cautious on the Sabbath Day,
With fervent prayers of Religion,
that we had passed away.
There was a football game between
the Béaraghs and the Kerrymen
T'would cheer the heart of anyone
To see that gallant play.

They played that noble game
for the space of sixty minutes past
A grander thing in history was never seen before
The Kerrys were victorious by one goal
And several winning points.
The Béaraghs from their boasting pride
fell back to murmuring shame.

Three cheers for Jerry Shea from Ardea
Our gallant Kerry boy,
Who played with force and energy
Along the marshy field
Dwyer Will O'Shea from the lakes
Followed backing him

They made an awful progress
Through the centre of the scene
Sullivan Green the tailor most experienced at football game.
That scored their goals for many a time bot active brave and keen
Bob Healy stood round guarding and warding off the enemy
They gave the chase of the Deer in hunt
To the boys of Sliav Ardgreem

Sullivan from Loughrea was the bravest man that stood the field
He is handsome tall genteel and straight
And right in all his parts
The Ladies were admiring him and his style of manly exercise
When the enemy came across his way, he kicked the ball at large, (felled them to
the ground)

When the Béaraghs had arrived they divided
Through the champion field
And stood awhile admiring all our boys of minor age
They had men from southern quarters,
Muintir Mhaire and Ros Carbery
A tailor from the Skellig Rock
The coward that sold his stage.

When the Béaraghs were defeated they came gliding through the champions
field.
To seek the sporting tavern to have a parting drain
I'm sure they were in need of it]Their teeth and jaws were trembling
With cheeks as pale as candle light and shedding tears like rain

Go back again you laymen to your cages in the wilderness
Wait another season 'till you science a little more,
You can eat your champion potatoes
Maiden rays and Pichey dogs
To strengthen up your muscles to play another goal.

We will plant the Laurel tree in that field to hail the memory
Of our brave and gallant Kerryboy
That won that struggling game
From Gluanhoo a true milesian King
That reigned in early centuries
The Kerry were descended in the
stain of Royal blood.

Collector: Mary Shea, Lehid
Informant: Patrick Shea

O'Sullivan Moore

Softly the sun shines to night o'er Dunkern.
Brightly it shines on the ruined castle wall.
Where once the great throng feasted so long and were merry
With O'Sullivan Moore in his banqueting hall.

But down by the seaside what means the loud murmur.
That sounds like the voice of an oncoming gale.
But Hark! it now rises in accents most awful
O laws! it's the sound of a wild Irish wail.

O'Sullivan Moore as he gazed on the water
One day when the summer sun brightly did shine
beheld so entrancing a fair female form.
And wished for his bride the fair maid from the brine.

So down to the seaside unheedingly resting.
And thoughtlessly swam to the female so fair.
But found not of earth was the creature before him
Oh! it was a mermaid alluring him there.

In vain did the chieftain attempt to return.
In vain did he struggle, no second was nigh.
And under the billows the mermaid had brought him.
Away from Dunkern to struggle and die.

Collector: Tom Harrington
Informant: George Harrington, father, aged 56

LANSDOWNE

Co. Ciarraí
Bar: Glenn an Ruachtaigh
Par: Tuaith Ó Siosta
Scoil: Lansdowne (Cuar na gCoileach)
Oide: Eibhlín Bean Ní Shúilleabháin

LANSDOWNE
Local Folklore and Stories

The Five Caileachs

Five old women lived happily together long ago named Purtam Portam, Caileach a Thartom, Caileach a Rúin, Caileach a Purpoon and Caileach a Thána. Well, once upon a time, when they had their grain cut saved and made into stacks, it happened that there were six stacks, one for each and one spare. They fell out and began to quarrel for the first time over the ownership of the sixth stack. "I'll have this," says Partam Portam. "No, you won't," says Caileach a Thartom. "I'll have it," says Caileach a Rúin. "Indeed, then you won't!" says Caileach a Purpoon. "But it is mine," says Caileach a Thána. They failed to come to any terms, and they spent a very uneasy night. At break of day they got ready by consent to go and lay their case before the King. After much deliberation these five old hags were received into his presence, and they told him their troubles. He advised them go home united and settle about dividing the odd stack into stooks. They were delighted and they thanked the King over and over for solving this riddle of theirs. They became fast friends and slept soundly that night. Next day they began at their stacks and divided them into stooks and a hard day's work it was. Finally, they finished the work but however they tried they had a stook over and the quarrel began as fresh as ever there and then. The very same dispute arose one word borrowing another until once again they went in the presence of the King who was both vexed and annoyed at seeing them back so soon again. The signs of disturbed minds showed clearly on their faces and they were quite as unreasonable as before. When he heard their tale of woe, he told them to clear out of his sight and not to come in his presence with any more such tales but to go home, like steady women, and to divide their stooks into sheaves, and then an odd sheaf wouldn't matter.

True they did as they were bade, but they returned the day after tomorrow asking his Majesty's pardon and begging him to listen to them. Though he felt very angry with them he ordered them home and told them to divide the odd sheaf into blades & to make the division evenly between them. This they did, but back they went as brazen as ever with the odd blade asking him for advice for the last time. The palace was situated on the seashore and casting the blade on the sea he said, "Ye have enough without it." Before he was able to finish his angry speech the the five old caileachs swam out to fetch the blade and were all drowned.

Collector: Eibhlín Bean Uí Shúilleabháin

LANSDOWNE
People, Places and Property

Bernard Shea

A man named Bernard Shea had a bakery in Kenmare long ago, seventy years ago perhaps. The bakers used come into the bakery late at night or rather in the small hours of the morning. The night in question his mother said is there water in for the bakers, Bernard? They found there was not there, and she sent himself and the maid across the street to the pump for a bath of water. The streets were then in complete darkness with no living soul abroad, and to their dismay they saw what appeared to be a woman almost flying down street towards them and where did she fall into but into their bath of water. "Oh! then," she said, as they stood there dumbfounded, "How late ye waited to bring in the water, the like of this didn't happen me since I left New York." Needless to say, they ran home for their lives and told their story leaving bath and water behind. It seemed quite incredible until a man in Market St, Kenmare got a message from Queenstown that his daughter who was on her way home from the States died on board ship and had to be thrown overboard.

Collector: Eibhlín Bean Uí Shúilleabháin

LANSDOWNE
History and Archaeology

Ogham Stones

There are three Ogham stones in Gleninchaquin about four miles from the main road and a holy well at which the folk paid rounds long ago & some did till lately as bits of shawls & ribbons hang around the bushes near it. And some cromlechs are still to be seen near Lohart ar thaobh an bóthair.

Collector: Eibhlín Bean Uí Shúilleabháin

LANSDOWNE
Songs

On Sheen's green banks in days of old

On Sheen's green banks in days of old
A dreadful fight was won.
The tale is by tradition told
Brought down from sire to son.

Two hostile tribes in fierce array
Drew near the chosen stream
Determined each to win the day
And win a glorious name
But ere the shout of war was rallied
A herald fast did ride
Proclaimed aloud to that great crowd
That night brave champions from
Each side the contest should decide.

Trúir 's a cúirear ón Seairc
Fear 's a react ó bóthar Neinín
Annsúd o'Paradar an cómhra cearc
Ar Inse Gaortaidh ar ais ar brúac na
Síon

The troops drew near at sound of horn
With murmurs rude and rife
And took their posts that sunny morn
To view the dreadful strife
With terrible shouts the battle raged
Reaching from each hill
While hand to hands the foes engaged
And quickly all was still

Seven at a side lay stretched in death
And one there wounded lay
And one unhurt and out of breath
Stood victor of the fray.
The dying man in accents weak
The survivor thus addressed

A drink a drink for mercy's sake
A drink my last request

With helmet doffed the warrior sped
And fetched it from the flood
For the base wretch though nearly dead
Was thirsting for his blood
When stooping o'er his fallen foe
Kind solace to impart
The villain aimed a dying blow
And stabbed him through the heart

The comrades of the dying man
Set up the war hoot cry
To take revenge they quickly ran
To take revenge or die.
Their enemies in full retreat
Fled for the mountain glen
Chased by a host urged on by hate
A host of furious men.

The slaughter lasted through the night
And few there did survive
To tell the story of that fight
For few there were alive.

On Sheen's green banks
The spot is shown
where this great fight took place,
And in the distance
Still well known the valley of the chase.

The Scairt men went back
to Bóid Eoghainís to take a creac
and the Bóid Eoghainís men followed
overtaking them at Brúac na Síon
where the fight took place.

Informant: Tadhg Díarmuide Ó Súilleabháin, aged 80

324

SHELBOURNE

Co. Ciarraí
Bar: Gleann an Ruachtaigh
Par: Neidín
Scoil: Siolbhrain
Oide: Sighle Bean Uí Thuama

SHELBOURNE
Local Folklore and Stories

St Finbar and the Serpent

St Finbar at first lived in a lonely cave in Valley Desmond. After some years he built a little church in the Island of Gougane. Every day he used to walk around the Island but never spoke to anyone. It is said that serpents frequented the lake and often did a lot of damage. One day he devoured a man and the saint happened to be present. He took out his book and prayed. The serpent appeared, vomited up the man, but the saint banished him from at the River Lee to Eve Leary, where he was found.

Informant: Nóra Ní Shuibhne, aged 32, Gurteen, Co. Kerry

The Enchanted Sunbeam

There lived in a remote part of the parish of Ballyvourney a Catholic boy who was never instructed in hie religious duties. At last, a travelling woman taught him his prayers and how to prepare for the sacraments. One Sunday he was preparing to go to Mass. A bright ray of sunshine came in at the window and stretched across the room. The boy, full of faith and innocence, threw his coat across the sunbeam, and it held the coat up, while the boy was getting ready to go to Mass. The second Sunday, he did the same, and the sunbeam held up the coat. The third Sunday, the boy had a new coat, and he thought how nice he would look at Mass, dressed up in his new suit. With these thoughts in his head, he threw the new coat across the sunbeam, but the sunbeam had lost all its charm before pride, and the new coat fell to the ground.

A Legend – St Abbie of Ballyvourney

It is said that when the people of Ballyvourney were in trouble, they used to go to St Gobnet for consolation and for advice. Once a poor old widow-woman was told that the Sheriff was coming to take her cattle. She went and told her story to the saint, but St. Gobnet told her not to worry, that her cattle could not be taken. When the men were collecting the cattle, the saint came with a hive of bees, and she shook them amongst the men who ran in every direction trying to escape. The more they ran, the more stings they got, and they were glad to beat off without the cattle.

Piseoga – Bainne

One night in Ballyvourney a priest was going on a sick call. He saw light in a graveyard but went on his way. When he was returning the light was still there, so he asked his boy to go with him to see who was there. When they came near the light, they saw an old woman lifting the lid of a coffin, cutting off the right hand off a corpse, and putting it into her apron. The priest asked her what she wanted the hand for, and she said she would take it home, put it under the cream-tub. When she would set the milk, she would dip the fingers of the hand into every keeler, and she would have that depth of cream in each keeler and would have firkins of butter for Cork market.

Piseog – Oíche Bhealtaine

In the old times a man was going home late from scoraecting, on May-night. A good distance from the road in a little hollow patch of ground he saw a light. He plucked up the courage and went to see what it was. As he went nearer, he saw an old woman spinning black wool. She used to spin for about five minutes, then her daughter used to undo all her mother's spinning, saying certain words at the same time. They continued this work till cockcrow, and this is how they managed to take their neighbours' butter for the year.

Informant: Nóra Ní Suibhne, aged 32, farmer, Gurteen, Co. Kerry

Scéal

There was once a woman who went with the fairies. Her husband was inquiring of everybody how he could get her back. A witch lived in the place, and she had knowledge of the fairies. The man went to her for advice, and she told him that all the fairies would be in the liss-field on May-night, and that she would give him certain signs and tokens whereby his wife would return to him. He did not trust the witch, so he went to the parish priest, and told him his story. The priest gave him a rod and a bottle of holy water. He told the man to go to the liss-field on May-night and to stand beside the liss. Then to stretch out the enchanted rod as far as it would go and to sprinkle the holy water in a ring around him. The man did this, and in the middle of the night the fairies came out, each riding a horse. His wife was on the seventh horse! They went round the ring of holy water. When his wife saw him, she jumped off her horse, and into the middle of the ring. All the other fairies are they passed round the ring said, "Tháinig sé chun sise d' fhagáil." [He came to leave her]. The man and his wife went home happily together.

Three races, a hound,
Three hounds a horse.
Three horses a man.
Three men a deer,
Three deer an eagle,
Three eagles a yew tree,
Three yew-trees an old ridge,
Three old ridges from the beginning to the end of the world.

Informant: Máire Ní Bhuachalla, aged 15, Coolnagoppoge, Co. Kerry
Informant: Seán Ó Buachalla, aged 50

Legend of Fiachna Graveyard

Long ago in the troubled times, eight men from Scairt, near Bantry, stole some cattle from Bórd Eoghainín near Caherdaniel. The cattle were soon missed, and eight strong brave men were sent in pursuit of them. They overtook them about a mile from this school, but the Bantry men refused to give back the cattle. It was decided that the sixteen men should have a fair fight. So, they selected a flat field - Ínse Gaorthadh Rais - on the banks of the River Sheen. The land is owned by Edward Egan, and the field is still pointed out. A terrible fight took place, in which they were all killed, except one from each side. One of these lay dying and he asked the other for a drink, but when the other was stooping down, he stabbed him to death. He then lay there all alone moaning piteously. At the same time some men were talking in a public-house in Kenmare about the seven remarkable bulláns, or round stones, in Fiachna Graveyard. They put up a bet that no one in Kenmare would go to the Bonane graveyard at midnight and bring down one of the seven bulláns. A girl in the house took up the challenge and set out. As she travelled along the Sheen, she heard the moaning at Ínse Gaorthadh Rais. Being very courageous, she went into the field, and saw that a man was lying there fatally wounded. He asked piteously for a drink, but the girl said she had no vessel to fetch it in. So, he told her to take off his shoe and to bring the water in it. She gave him a drink and he had barely strength to say, "Bíodh an chreach agat." [Have the prey]. She collected the cattle and drove them home. It is supposed that this incident saved the girl's life, as she never went to Fiachna. The bulláns are enchanted, and if she attempted to steal one, she would be in the power of the fairies for the rest of her life.

Collector: Gobnet O' Connell, aged 15, Dromanassig, Co. Kerry
Informant: John O' Connell, aged 49

SHELBOURNE
People, Places and Property

James Grady

When the soup was given out in Kenmare, the OMahony's of Dromore were at the head of it. One day when O'Mahony was giving a speech at the square, a young man named James Grady jumped on the platform and caught Mahony by the collar of the coat, and pulled him off the platform, and then fled. Father John O'Sullivan was then Parish Priest of Kenmare, so James Grady went to his house to hide from the police who were in search of him. Father John gave him permission to stay with him as long as he liked. That night when they were preparing for bed, they heard a loud knock at the door. "Who is there?" asked Father John. "Policemen in search of one James Grady," said the men outside. The priest then told Grady to stand his ground, and not to be afraid. Father John took out his book and read over Grady. Then he opened the door, and the policemen came in. Although Grady was sitting beside the fire, the searchers never saw him, and they went away quite satisfied that he was not at the priest's house. Grady remained there for a few days and when he was leaving Father John told him that he could walk around the town of Kenmare, and that no policeman would lay a hand on him. He did as he was told no policeman was able to see him.

Informant: Máire Ní Bhuachalla, aged 13, Coolnagoppoge, Co.
Kerry
Informant: Seán Ó Buachalla, aged 60

SHELBOURNE
Local Customs

An Bhrídeog

In the Parish of Tuogh it is an old-time custom to make a Biddy for St Bridget's Night. The Biddy is built on a churn-staff, so that the figure can stand on the table. She is dressed in white, wearing a blue sash. For a head a large turnip is shaped, carved and painted by a handy man. Some flax is kept from year to year and stuck on for hair. A large cross is made and sewn on to her left shoulder. When finished she looks quite real. On St Bridget's Night a crowd collects, and one is selected to carry the Biddy, the others march, accompanied by music. They go about from house to house, place the Biddy on the table, she is welcomed by the bean a' tige. There is a round of music and dancing in each house.

History and Archaeology

Teampall Fiachna

In the parish of Bonane, on the old road from Kenmare to Bantry, stands St Fiachna's Graveyard, still in use. All that now remains of the Church, which was eighty feet long and twenty feet wide, is the eastern gable, now fifteen feet high at the apse, and traces of the remaining walls nowhere more than three feet in height. A jungle of shrub, weeds, and ivy cover the ruin, but in spite of this the sanctity is still maintained, and in the eastern gable where a stone had become displaced, somebody has placed a china figure of Our Lady and the Holy Child with other emblems of devotion. On the opposite side of the road to the graveyard there is a path through a field which leads to a small holy well - Tobar Fiachna, protected over by large boulders. On the top of these boulders lies a flat stone, having a pebble alongside it, with which those making the rounds of the well scratch on the stone the sign of the cross. Many cures were affected at this well, but it is said that was especially remarkable was curing rheumatism.

Legend of Fiachna

It is said that a certain woman every night milked the cows of her neighbours and transferred milk to her own dairy. Suspected at length, the hue and cry was raised against her, and St Fiachna, who led a holy life at the church resolved to punish the woman. He mounted his horse to visit her, but she fled. The saint, as he passed, turned her dairy into stone. and then descended the hill towards the river in pursuit of her. He crossed the stream and rode up the opposite hillside, where about mid-way he overtook the criminal of whom he was in chase, and instantly turned her into stone, and there she still stands, a good gallán of six feet in height. The woman carried a spancel in her hand, with a búircín at the end of it. She used to spancel the cows while milking. From the búircín of the spancel a tree grew up in the bare hillside. Some people say that the saint had a sword in his hand when he followed the milk stealer, and after crossing the stream, and going up the opposite side of the valley, she being close before him, he made a slash at her with his sword. He missed her, however, but in doing so, cut into two halves a large boulder, still to be seen - and after that he called on God to turn the woman into stone. There she still stands, intended by the good St. Fiachna to be an awful warning to thieves.

The Petrified Dairy

In St Fiachna's Graveyard, on the roadside, stands a large roughly rectangular boulder; the top and sides being flat, the front erect and perpendicular, and the back sunk in the soil. The top of the block resembles a table and it is about six feet square with the corners facing the four cardinal points. On the surface there are hollowed out seven large bulláns or rock basins, undoubtedly artificially arranged, as shown in the accompanying scale-plan. Each bullán is about one foot in diameter, and five inches deep, having nearly vertical sides and a slightly rounded base. In each of the seven bulláns there lies a smooth, rounded and oval-shaped stone, of a size suitable to that of the inside of the basin. Rainwater fills each hollow round the contained stone. This big boulder is known as the Petrified Dairy, indicated as such by its seven keeler, and seven pats of butter, one in each keeler. These pebbles should never be removed from the keelers, or some misfortune may befall the person who does so. It is said that a man took one pebble home to cure a sick cow, and that before morning all his cows were dead in the cabin and that the pebble taken, came back of itself and rested again in its own keeler.

The Rock of the Warts

At the present time there is another use of the dairy of quite a different character. It is said that rounds are paid there for curing warts. The person affected with warts must go round the rock seven times in the direction contrary to the path of the sun. He must say an Our Father and Hail Mary at each of the basins, dip his finger into the water under the stone, rub the water on the warts, making the Sign of the Cross on them, and in two months they will be gone.

Informant: Mícheál Ó Tuama, aged 76, farmer, Kenmare, Co. Kerry

MacCarthy's Gallant Son

In the time of the Fenians, the Kenmare people suffered a great deal at the hands of the invaders. A brave band of Bonane Volunteers drilled and fought under the leadership of Jeremiah McCarthy of Tullaha, Kenmare. Unfortunately, there was a spy in the ranks, one O'Sullivan, but the people nicknamed him An Báille Galldha. One night after they had been informed upon by the Báille Galldha, the English soldiers surrounded the house of young McCarthy at Tullaha. The wanted youth was sleeping peacefully in his bedroom, but when he heard them, he jumped out through the back window, breaking sash and frame, and made his way to the Sheen River, swam across, and made his escape to Bantry. The following are a few verses from a ballad composed by one of his own men

MacCarthy's Gallant Son

Through hill and glen, they marched and drilled,
When shone the rising moon,
Their hearts with hopes for Ireland filled,
To burst her fetters soon.
Brave-hearted, bold and fleet were they,
And dauntless everyone,
But the fleetest one of all, they say,
Was McCarthy's gallant son.
The Peelers round his dwelling, drawn,
While slept poor Mac serene
But soon he awoke and bested them,
And 'cleared the River Sheen.

Killowen – The Battle of Whitehouse

About two miles from Kenmare is the townland of Killowen, and situated on one of the many headlands jutting out in to the sea, is seen a mass of ruins of the White House. Sir William Petty, ancestor of Lord Landsdowne, obtained extensive estates for surveying after the Rebellion of 1641. He planted a colony of English Protestants at Killowen. These were attacked in 1688 by the Irish and took refuge in the White House, the residence of Petty's agent, and unable to withstand the siege they surrendered. Mr Richard Orpen, agent for Petty's property, and the Rev. Thomas Palmer were managers of the colony. They petitioned General Justin McCarthy and Sir Valentine Browne, Governor of Kerry, to deal with the Irish, and they were told to bring in the villains, but this they could not do. The houses of the petitioners were attacked, and they feared for their lives. Mr Palmer's first wife was a relation of Sir Richard Alworth who lived in Newmarket. He told them to go to Bandon and to bring their provisions and horses with them. They were afraid with only a dozen horses to travel that stretch of savage country. They stayed where they were in the White House - 44ft long, 22 ft wide and 2½ storeys high. Four large rooms and garret stood on rock, the tide flowed almost around it and they enclosed a half-acre of ground surrounded by a wall 14 ft. high and 12 ft. thick. All promised to obey Orpen and Palmer and to hold the place for King William. McCarthy and Browne favoured King James and didn't give much help. The Irish besieged the place and offered very favourable terms for surrender, but the besieged would not accept these terms but after a while they had to. The garrison were shipped off to England. Orpen had to go to Cork and from that he went to England, and they were all kept by Lady Shelbourne.

Ardea Castle

There is a local tradition that this castle was built with the blood of man and beast. When the last stone is razed to the ground Ireland will be free. The sea is gradually wearing the ruins away. Ten miles to the aouthwest of Kenmare stands the ruins of Ardea Castle. Some say Moriartys owned it and other say O'Donoghues. Legend says that the last of the O'Donoghues passed into Loc Léin and on the anniversary of passing Lá Bealtaine, he is to be seen riding over the hills on a white horse. His spirit is not supposed to rest until the last stone of Ardea Castle is removed. In 1641, Rununci, the Papal Legate, landed at Ardea and was entertained in the castle. He passed on to Ardtully Castle (through Inbhear Scéine and the Roughty River), the residence of Finian McCarthy Mór.

Collector: Máire Ní Ailgheasa, Gortnacurra, Co. Kerry

SHELBOURNE
Songs

The Nun of Sweet Kenmare

Farewell to my acquaintances,
and to my native land!
Farewell to all my comrade dear,
with all my heart and hand.
My mind is like a wandring wave,
That shuffles to and fro.
To leave my parents fond behind,
In sorrow, grief and woe.

O! Erin, dear, my native soil,
Where is the land so brave,
That reared such graceful daughters
They are all beyond the wave;
Their Substance is all plundered.
By landlords' tyranny;
O! Erin dear, my hearts delight.
I long to see thee free.

Farewell to County Kerry,
for 'tis there I do reside;
'Tis from it that all Irishmen
first raised their heads with pride.
It reared brave Dan that led them on
The British laws he tore.
Ó grá mo croi, I long to see.
Old Ireland free once more!

Farewell to sweet Killarney,
its lakes and towering peaks,
Mangerton's lofty,
and the MaGillicuddy's Reeks;
Where the deer and doe do skip and go.

.

O'er woodland, hill, and dale,
Where the eagles soar and the torrents
roar,
On the shores of sweet loc léin!

Farewell to sweet Kenmare,
Its church and convent grand,
It has won great admiration,
In every foreign land;
That pious noble lady,
sister Mary Frances Clare,
She is remembered in all nations.
She is the Nun of Sweet Kenmare.

Farewell to sweet Kilgarvan,
Crossroads and back to Sneem,
Up to Glengariff Tunnel,
And along the winding Sheen!
Where lovers do take pleasure,
And there do roam each day,
From Gulliba's romantic hills,
And back to Kenmare Bay!

I now must stop my wandering pen,
As the ship at anchor lies,
To plough the broad Atlantic wave,
To Columbia of the free:
When I think upon my native land,
And none to it can compare.
So adieu to all for evermore,
And to the nun of sweet Kenmare

Collector: Máighréid Ní Shúilleabháin, aged 14, Coolnagoppoge
Informant: Séamus Ó Súilleabháin, aged 68

Kate Dhíarmáin

One pleasant morning in the month of August,
As I chanced to walk down by the Roughty side,
The birds were warbling, their notes were charming,
The sun was warm and very bright.

I heard a wailing of lamentation,
Poor Dan complaining to old Diarmáin,
How he was forsaken by lovely Katie,
And she was going out lately to Laca Bán.

To hear him calling, he was crying and bawling,
The tears were falling down from his eyes.
And saying both father and bouncing daughter,
Are full of "palaver," and very shy.

Oh? Patsy Cronin, I won't be joking,
I'm too long controlling this heavy spite,
To hunt and rattle and kill your cattle,
I cut a wattle the other nigh

This was composed by a man, who lived in Inchees, named John A. Twomey R.I.C. for a man who was disappointed in love. This poet is dead for the past twelve or thirteen years. These are other verses he composed for the lady "Kate Dhiarmáin."

Kate is as straight as a poker,
On Sunday she goes like a fawn,
The Gaelic is able to stroke her,
And send her back home to Dhiarmáin.

How simply I styled him The Gaelic,
Not wishing his name to be known,
He is the roving patrolling old Gaelic,
That stepped on the tail of his gown.

What race of dark knaves are those Cronins
That live down below Laca Bán,
How strange and how quare are those notions!
In taking these folks to Gouganne!

Long Katie was there in good order,
She was like and Commander in Chief,
Oh faith, she was wearing red garters,
And things that looked awful to me.

Collector: Máighréad Ní Thuama, aged 26, Teacher, Gortlahard
Informant: Seán Ó Tuama, aged 60

The Buck from Bonane

You lads and gay lasses, I claim your attention,
Until I will tell you what happened to those,
Who left Ballingeary on the 15th of August,
And went over to Borland in search of a goat.

They travelled Coom Ruadh, and the south side of Maolagh,
To Faillatureen, and to sweet Leaca Bán,
The heights of Moing More
And the wild cliffs of Borland,
And they never cried stop till they came to Bonane.

And when they had seen him,
They thought him most pleasing,
Says Carty to Sheehan get fast in his throat.
Cotter and Creedon, then ran most briskful,
And soon on his horns they placed a thick rope.

And when they had caught him,
For home they then started,
No doubt they were dry when they came to Gougane.
They placed this bold hers, quite safe in a car-house,
And drank to the health of the Buck from Bonane.

And when they came out after drinking some porter,
In Cronin's hotel in lonely Gougane,
Then they went to the car-house,
To take out this wild ranger,
No doubt he was then half-ways to Bonane.

They all began shouting and loudly bewailing
And the company all began for to sigh,
Saying we must look out for some other bold hero,
Or the goats of our place, they will surely run dry.

When the buck got his liberty out of the car-house,
He cocked up his tail, and puffed with his nose.
And ran back the field like any young racehorse
Thanking Mike Healy for letting him go.

When he found himself safe in the wild cliffs of Maolagh,
He took up his head, and it was then he spoke.
Saying, "Good-bye,",Ballingeary, until the next season.
You'll ne'er see me again, nor neither the rope.

He slept west in Maolach, that night in a bailic;
For he thought it too late to go home.
And early next morning he started for Borland,
No doubt he was laughing when he thought of his course.

On coming backwards, he met the young Tacker,
Saying where have you been my rogue?
I have been carried east by those wild Ballingeary's,
To earn for them both silver and gold.

As I spoke of this ranger 'tis time I should praise him,
I will tell you his age, it was scarcely eighteen.
His size was enormous, well-shaped and well-formed.
And beautifully armed with horns indeed.

His eyes they were shining, like two sparkling diamonds.
His magairlí so fine hanging down on his knees,
With age he was brown, though his limbs they were sound,
And also in his mouth was a set of good teeth.

So now my brave boys some advice I will give you,
If you are ever in search of a goat,
Go back to Bonane, and find the right owner,
And pay him cash down, both silver and gold.

And when you are coming home.
Don't drink any porter,
But leave someone to care him in lonely Gougane,
So now, in conclusion, I think I'll give over,
And I'll sing no more of this Buck from Bonane.

The Vale of Lackaroe

Now Captain Daniel Murphy
was a ranting roving boy,
His head was lined with music,
and his heart was lined with joy,
His head was all a lump of pluck,
As all the heroes know,
But his heart belongs to Eily,
She is the pride of Lackaroe.

When the Captain was a bailiff,
He was sitting by a pool,
The harvest moon was shining
And the night was calm and cool,
He was softly wandering,
and his soul was fancy free,
When he saw Miss Eilly coming
With a bag of bannakeen.

In this case, then, said the Captain,
You can poison all you like.
And I'll run up the village,
For a stroke-all and a pike
We'll bag a dozen salmon,
And no one will it know,
And we'll take them
to your father's cottage,
In the Vale of Lackaroe.

This seagull was so secret,
Sure no one saw the light,
The Captain and Miss Eily,
They are lovers since that night
The blessings of a marriage,
They very soon shall know,
And they both shall live so happily
In the Vale of Lackaroe

SOURCES

INDEX

9 781036 905767